Analysing Conversation

Rules and Units
in the Structure of Talk

LANGUAGE & COMMUNICATION LIBRARY

Series Editor: Roy Harris, *University of Oxford*

A Related Pergamon Journal

Language & Communication*

An Interdisciplinary Journal
Editor: Roy Harris, *University of Oxford*

The primary aim of the journal is to fill the need for a publicational forum devoted to the discussion of topics and issues in communication which are of interdisciplinary significance. It will publish contributions from researchers in all fields relevant to the study of verbal and non-verbal communication. Emphasis will be placed on the implications of current research for establishing common theoretical frameworks within which findings from different areas of study may be accommodated and interrelated.

By focusing attention on the many ways in which language is integrated with other forms of communicational activity and interactional behaviour it is intended to explore ways of developing a science of communication which is not restricted by existing disciplinary boundaries.

*Free specimen copy available on request.

NOTICE TO READERS

Dear Reader

An invitation to Publish in and Recommend the Placing of a Standing Order to Volumes Published in this Valuable Series

If your library is not already a standing/continuation order customer to this series, may we recommend that you place a standing/continuation order to receive immediately upon publication all new volumes. Should you find that these volumes no longer serve your needs, your order can be cancelled at any time without notice.
The Editors and the Publisher will be glad to receive suggestions of outlines of suitable titles, reviews or symposia for editorial consideration: if found acceptable, rapid publication is guaranteed.

ROBERT MAXWELL
Publisher at Pergamon Press

Analysing Conversation

Rules and Units
in the Structure of Talk

by

TALBOT J. TAYLOR
College of William & Mary, Virginia, USA

and

DEBORAH CAMERON
Roehampton Institute, London, UK

PERGAMON PRESS
OXFORD · NEW YORK · BEIJING · FRANKFURT
SÃO PAULO · SYDNEY · TOKYO · TORONTO

U.K.	Pergamon Press, Headington Hill Hall, Oxford OX3 0BW, England
U.S.A.	Pergamon Press, Maxwell House, Fairview Park, Elmsford, New York 10523, U.S.A.
PEOPLE'S REPUBLIC OF CHINA	Pergamon Press, Room 4037, Qianmen Hotel, Beijing, People's Republic of China
FEDERAL REPUBLIC OF GERMANY	Pergamon Press, Hammerweg 6, D-6242 Kronberg, Federal Republic of Germany
BRAZIL	Pergamon Editora, Rua Eça de Queiros, 346, CEP 04011, Paraiso, São Paulo, Brazil
AUSTRALIA	Pergamon Press Australia, P.O. Box 544, Potts Point, N.S.W. 2011, Australia
JAPAN	Pergamon Press, 8th Floor, Matsuoka Central Building, 1-7-1 Nishishinjuku, Shinjuku-ku, Tokyo 160, Japan
CANADA	Pergamon Press Canada, Suite No. 271, 253 College Street, Toronto, Ontario, Canada M5T 1R5

Copyright © 1987 T. J. Taylor and D. Cameron

First edition 1987

Library of Congress Cataloging in Publication Data
Taylor, Talbot J.
Analysing conversation.
Bibliography: p.
Includes index.
1. Conversation.   2. Oral communication.
I. Cameron, Deborah.   II. Title.
P95.45.T39   1987   001.54'2   86-30620

Taylor, Talbot J.
Analysing conversation: rules and units
in the structure of talk.— (Language &
communication library)
1. Conversation
I. Title   II. Cameron, Deborah   III. Series
808.56   P95.45
ISBN 0-08-033362-1

Printed in Great Britain by A. Wheaton & Co. Ltd., Exeter

Acknowledgements

This book is the fruit of a combined total of more than ten years' research by the authors. We would like to thank our editor, Roy Harris, for the advice and encouragement he has given us throughout this period; we are also grateful to Peter Mühlhäusler, Liz Frazer and to our fellow graduate students in linguistics at Oxford in the early 1980s. Talbot Taylor's contribution has been partially supported by grants from Trinity College Oxford and the College of William & Mary, Williamsburg. We acknowledge the assistance of those institutions with thanks.

Although both authors shared in the germination and development of this book's central ideas and arguments, each of us bears primary responsibility (and blame) for certain chapters in particular. Talbot Taylor is responsible for Chapters 2, 5, 6 and 7; Deborah Cameron for Chapters 1, 3, and 4. Parts of Chapter 7 have already appeared in *Language and Communication*, Vol. 4, No. 2 (1984).

T.J.T.
D.C.

Contents

1

Introduction: Rules and Units

In the last fifteen years the analysis of conversation has become one of the most active and fastest developing fields in the study of language and communication. In this time countless articles and books have been written extolling the virtues of this or that model of conversational organization.

However, although one or two surveys of the field have recently appeared, these have, on the whole, refrained from adopting a critical perspective. Perhaps the analysis of conversation has seemed too young and as yet too unstable to merit a comprehensive, critical account of its overall strengths and weaknesses. Perhaps it has been thought better to allow conversation analysts a period of grace, in order to see where their foundational assumptions lead, rather than criticize before the field has had time to establish itself. In any case, no general critical assessment of the analysis of conversation as a semi-institutionalized domain of enquiry has yet been published. Our intention is to break this pattern. We believe the time has come for a critical survey of the concepts and methods of conversation analysis (an expression we use to mean the study of the organization of conversational interaction, whatever the analyst's theoretical orientation; we do not restrict the term *conversation analysis* to ethnomethodological studies like those described in Chapter 6 below).

In fact, this book is far from being a complete survey of the field of conversation analysis: we have only been able to deal with a small selection of the models currently popular, although we do feel our selection is representative of the major trends and schools of thought in the field. But what is more important is that we have severely limited the focus of our account to an investigation of the applications of two fundamental assumptions shared by all the models we consider. The first of these assumptions is that conversations consist, at least in part, in the production of particular sorts of interactional units, such as speech acts, or moves, or turns, or sentences, etc. The second assumption is that in producing these units, conversationalists are guided by interactional rules which determine when particular units may occur, how they may be recognized, what they may be combined with, and generally, how they fit into the organizational structure of a conversation.

It might well be asked *why* we have decided to focus on the use of rules and units in conversation analysis. One reason is that every version of conversation analysis we know of makes some use of these notions (or variants of them). Thus in the next five chapters we will demonstrate in detail that various superficially quite distinct approaches resemble each other in their overall conception. The models we examine are those of the social psychologists (Chapter 2), 'speech act' theorists (Chapter 3), and 'exchange structure' analysts of the Birmingham school (Chapter 4); a Gricean approach based on principles and maxims (Chapter 5) and ethnomethodological conversation analysis (Chapter 6). We will be concerned not only with the resemblances between models, but also with their differing ideas about rules and units: how they conceptualize these two key notions; how they justify the epistemological adequacy of the rules and units approach; how they analyse data in terms of their assumptions about rules and units; what they take the ontological status of rules and units to be.

In addition, our focus on rules and units allows us to raise more general questions, and to cast some light on some of the most salient issues in the contemporary study of language and communication. For instance: is communicative interaction governed by rules (tacitly) known to all interactants? And if it is rule governed, *how* is it rule governed? Why do communicators follow the rules? Or, to put it differently, how do the rules inform their production of behaviour? Furthermore, how do communicators know if co-communicators are following the same rules they are? These questions about the intersubjectivity of rules suggest similar ones about the intersubjectivity of units: do communicators identify the same conversational units in behaviour, and if so, how do they bring off such a shared identification? Is it a matter of reason, of convention, of habit, or experience, or what? Now is the time, we feel, to address general questions such as these to conversation analysis as a field. As we argue later on, in our conclusion (Chapter 8), the answers are crucial not only to linguistics and the study of human communication, but to all the human and social sciences. Our aim in the remainder of this introductory chapter is to place the rules and units approach in its general intellectual context, giving some indication of the questions and problems which will recur in our later, more detailed, discussions.

The emergence of a rules and units approach in conversation analysis

Conversation analysis is an interdisciplinary concern: major contributions have been made by philosophers, psychologists, sociologists and linguists. Yet the rules and units framework which, we claim, informs them all, is perhaps especially typical of linguistic models. Its preoccupations are with segmentation, classification and combination. Types and tokens, syntagms and paradigms—these are the classic concerns of descriptive and structural grammar, and they are present to a high degree in most currently influential approaches to conversation.

It is probably significant that the earliest attempts to model discourse and conversation in a systematic way were made precisely by American structuralist linguists in the 1950s: Zellig Harris and Kenneth Pike. Harris, in his article 'Discourse analysis' (1952), tried to extend the strict formal principle of distributional analysis to stretches longer than a single sentence (his data were mostly textual, as opposed to conversational). He was able to set up discourse 'equivalence classes' which captured generalizations about sequential and co-occurrence restrictions in a specific text, but not to say anything more general about discourse, nor to make illuminating syntagmatic predictions (Harris, 1970, p. 373). Pike (1967) similarly extended his 'tagmemic' grammatical model to analyse larger units, including conversations. He invented a unit-type, the 'behavioreme' or 'uttereme', discussing its structure and its boundaries at length; unlike Harris, his approach to analysis was not formal but functional, and he attempts a general 'slot and filler' account of talk.

These were the first rules and units models (though typically, more concerned with units than rules). So obscure, or bizarre, are they considered today that it is rare for either to be discussed in any detail (and in Pike's case, even a citation is rare). Yet contemporary models in their various ways instantiate principles not dissimilar to theirs.

The early work of Pike and Harris apart, it is probably true to say that the major impetus for the study of conversation has tended to come from outside linguistics. Conversation as an object of linguistic study was recommended, characteristically, by J. R. Firth: 'It is here,' he observed in 'The technique of semantics' (1957, p. 32), 'that we shall find the key to a better understanding of what language really is and how it works.' But in the mainstream of linguistic description conversation was marginalized: the features typical of conversational interaction (ungrammaticality, discontinuity, context-dependence, interactivity) were idealized, which is to say ignored, by the Saussurean and Chomskyan paradigms with their insistence on studying *langue* or competence. When conversational organization became, quite recently, a respectable area for linguistic research, a great deal of work had already been done by speech act theorists working in philosophy, social psychologists and ethnomethodologists.

Paradoxically, however, these other social scientists had in the meantime been influenced, and in some cases inspired, by the prestige and success of Chomskyan linguistics. While not necessarily accepting the whole of Chomsky's philosophy or indeed his methodological strictures, social scientists were attracted by the notion of reducing human behaviour to sets of (preferably elegant) generative rules. The attraction is especially noticeable in their rhetoric: Goffman says enthusiastically of Garfinkel, for instance, that he

> . . . extended the argument by going on to look for rules which, when followed, allow us to generate a world of a given kind. To uncover the informing, constitutive rules of everyday life would be to perform the sociologist's alchemy (Goffman, 1974, p. 5).

On one level, what a quotation like this one demonstrates is the confusion and eclecticism in social scientists' responses: 'constitutive rules' are a concept familiar from speech act theory, rule-*following* is a Wittgensteinian concept, foreign to generative linguistics. But there is a clear general approval for some kind of rule-based model, and that approval frequently finds support from the specific example of generative grammar.

The interdisciplinary field of conversation analysis which has developed over the last fifteen years is extremely complex and heterogeneous. It would be misleading to view its burgeoning literature as a chronological or linear development from some common impulse or seminal work, in part because of the roots of its practitioners in several quite different academic disciplines. Nevertheless, it is possible to discern certain key themes in conversational analysis, and these may be outlined briefly here.

The first major theme—and it is one which we in the present study are only tangentially concerned with—is usually given the disciplinary label *pragmatics*. It focuses on the interpretation of utterances and on how an account of this aspect of language use may be incorporated into a more general grammatical model. Historically, it is in connexion with the issue of utterance interpretation that we find speech act theory being taken up seriously by mainstream linguists, notably by the generative semanticists (see, for example, Ross (1970), Gordon and Lakoff (1971), Sadock (1974), Cole and Morgan (1975)). The authors of these studies were not simple descriptivists with an interest in conversation *per se*: rather, they sought to show that the scope of generative syntax could, indeed should, be extended to model phenomena previously defined as 'performance'. While the judgement of history seems to have been that they took this extension to inordinate lengths (Newmeyer, 1980), it is ultimately to this line of work that we may trace the new developments in linguistic pragmatics exemplified by 'relevance theory' (Sperber and Wilson, 1986). Relevance theory focuses on utterance interpretation and assumes a 'modular' approach to grammar: the generative semanticists were also interested in utterance interpretation and how it could be integrated into a grammatical model.

Work in speech act theory and in generative semantics can be seen to have some of the preoccupations of the rules and units approach. For the generative semanticists it was very natural to think of regularities and constraints on behaviour in terms of rules: theirs was literally a grammatical model. Whereas the nature of Austin's and Searle's speech act framework very strongly encouraged a preoccupation with taxonomy—that is, with segmenting and classifying units. Descriptive essays in the Austin/Searle tradition, such as Labov and Fanshel's *Therapeutic Discourse* (1977), would situate themselves far more firmly in the arena of conversation analysis (as opposed to that of pragmatics or generative grammar); we shall have much more to say about them later in this book.

The second theme which needs to be mentioned is again one about which we shall have rather little to say: it is often referred to under the heading of 'ethnography of speaking'. The ethnographic approach, used extensively by sociologists, anthropologists and sociolinguists, is far less constrained by the rules and units framework (though some analysts have chosen to formulate their observations in a quasi-grammatical rule format, a well-known instance being Labov's 'Rules for ritual insults' (1972)).

Ethnography of speaking seeks to describe the typical features of varied speech events; to catalogue features of speaker, addressee, setting, topic, channel and the like. Insofar as it does use the notion of 'rule', this approach tends to focus on societal *conventions* for the use of certain types of expression or the performance of particular speech acts—as we shall argue later on in this chapter, this is quite a different perspective on rules from the one which is characteristic of, say, social psychological models. Nevertheless, ethnographers do very frequently regard talk as a rule-governed activity; and they may also concern themselves with classifying speech acts, which implies a complementary interest in taxonomy.

The third current we can identify in the analysis of conversation is one which emphasizes conversational *structure*; which seeks, that is, to describe conversation as a distinctive, highly organized level of language. It is to this current that we will devote most of our attention.

What, precisely, is 'conversational structure'? Clearly, the phrase trades on our everyday intuition that conversation is neither aimless nor random, that on the contrary it exhibits regularity and pattern. For example, as the ethnomethodologists have pointed out, many commonplace features of talk display 'precision timing' and orderliness where one might in principle expect chaos (the classic example being turn-exchange). Interlocutors standardly 'know what to expect' in various sorts of talk and manage to meet, on indefinitely many occasions, acceptable standards of relevance and politeness (they answer questions; they recognize greetings; they inform each other of things; and so on). The result is co-operative and non-bizarre talk, quite often involving the repetition of extremely predictable sequences.

The decision that this kind of pattern or 'structure' should be described in terms of rules and units seems in many cases to have been arrived at almost by default: the rules and units framework is familiar enough to seem natural. As Michael Stubbs remarks (1981, p. 101), 'one would expect at least some of the same kinds of patterning in discourse as elsewhere in language'. This comment gives us a clear indication of what, specifically, is meant by talking about conversational structure: it is, as Stubbs has also observed, 'the surface distribution of forms' (1981, p. 107). From this standpoint, the task of the analyst is a straightforward descriptive one which falls into two parts, roughly speaking: first, the forms themselves must be identified, the basic components from which talk is constructed, and then it is necessary to examine their patterning, which in spoken discourse means primarily the way they are sequenced.

So far we have made the structural analysis of conversation sound narrowly structural*ist* in the manner of Pike or Harris, a matter of plotting mere distribution. And certainly, that element in a great many models should not be ignored or underestimated. But there are variations on the basic theme. Since conversation is a joint production, so its characteristic structured sequences are also produced jointly. We can ask, then, what underlying principles must be shared by conversationalists for successful, well-structured communication to occur. Can the organized and regular nature of conversation be *explained* as well as *described*? A number of analysts have gone beyond merely cataloguing regularities to posit that the descriptive formulae which capture or reproduce such regularities are actually known and used by conversationalists. Again, this is an idea that comes naturally to linguists working in a post-Chomskyan discipline: it also means that the models discussed in this book, while they may be in a similarly structural paradigm, are rather more ambitious than Harris's or Pike's.

The approaches which have emerged in the last few years as central to conversational analysis have all been influenced to some extent by the idea of behaviour as structured and rule-governed, and on many the influence of structural and generative linguistics has been particularly strong. Problems of segmentation and classification on one hand, and of behavioural regularity and predictability on the other, have been perceived by analysts as equally relevant to 'lower' and 'higher' levels of linguistic analysis. But how exactly do we formulate those problems in the specific domain of *conversational* structure? As a preliminary to the case-studies which form the main part of this book, we turn now to the general issues surrounding rules and units of conversation.

Rules

The idea that human behaviour may be described or explained in terms of rules is familiar to analysts of conversation from two main sources. One of these is the social scientific tradition which draws on Wittgenstein's later philosophy (for an influential reading, see Winch (1958)); the other is specific to modern linguistics and is associated in particular with the notion of *grammar*. Both traditions use the concept of a rule to capture observed regularities of behaviour, but in other ways they diverge quite sharply and may even be considered incompatible with one another. The models of conversation to be considered in this book have drawn on both traditions, to differing extents, and it is therefore important to consider each one more closely.

Social science: followable prescriptions

The notions of rule and rule-governed behaviour have been crucial to the recent development of the social sciences (centrally, sociology and psychology) and for the philosophy of social science. What the notions actually mean for a researcher interested in human behaviour is summed up by Harré (1974, p. 143):

> The method by which human beings manage their affairs, and create society, is by the invention and promulgation of rules in the following of which social behaviour is generated.

A rule is a precept which social actors follow, or else choose to flout. Although its function for the social scientist is similar to a rule of grammar's function for a linguist, in that it allows one to account for regularities of behaviour, in linguist's terms the social scientist's rule is *prescriptive*, since it is used to guide conduct rather than being a hypothesis *about* conduct.

Historically, this conception of a rule marks a break with the idea of the natural *law*, and thus with the tradition of the natural sciences and their notions of causality. According to proponents of the rule approach, the regularities of behaviour are quite unlike those of nature, since the former result from willed acts of individuals, while the latter embody a physical or logical necessity (Winch, 1958, p. 88). Put in plain language, it is possible to violate a rule, but not a law.

The argument for rules in social science, however, goes rather further than this. It is not just that regularities exist which are not the result of physical or logical necessity. Analysts such as Shimanoff (1980) also observe that deviations from a rule may occasion negative sanctions, and that behaviour is typically both criticizable (i.e. other social actors can say why and how it is inappropriate) and controllable. It is also contextual, in that criticisms and judgements are tied to particular occasions, but recur in situations that resemble each other. All these points suggest that a rule is a *social* norm, meaningful only within certain social arrangements.

This concept of a rule is incompatible with the traditional goal of scientific prediction, since normativity and causality are not at all the same thing. Winch remarks (1958, p. 94):

> The central concepts that belong to our understanding of social life are incompatible with the concepts central to the activity of scientific prediction. When we speak of the possibility of scientific prediction of social developments . . . we literally do not understand what we are saying. We cannot understand it, because it has no sense.

Nevertheless, a rule-based account can qualify as 'scientific' if not in the old sense of making causal or predictive statements, at least in the sense of giving principled explanations (Harré, 1974, p. 146). The social rule, a 'followable prescription', thus becomes the social scientific equivalent of the natural law; and the assumption that social scientists are doing something more than just informally (if insightfully) describing single events is saved, in spite of their inability to make predictions.

Within this framework of rule-based description, what would constitute explanation? If the rules are envisaged as prescriptive, matters to be explained might include how they are learned, and how actors make choices about whether or not to follow them. There is also the question of why a given rule is there in the first place. This is not always addressed by analysts who favour rules: Brown and Levinson point out (1978, p. 287) that for many, the mere statement of a rule is 'the terminal point of investigation', and they suggest that this may inhibit the search for generalization beyond the particular data being described. They themselves have looked for the sources of patterned behaviour in notions of 'goals' and 'rationality'. This also appears to be part of Harré's project, in which

> A human is treated as a person, that is a plan-making self-monitoring agent, aware of goals and deliberately considering the best ways of achieving them (Harré, 1974, p. 148).

Brown and Levinson (1978) postulate universal goals or rational desires (e.g. to be well regarded, or not to be imposed on) to which an analyst might refer in motivating all the multifarious, culturally variable strategies that exist for being polite, relevant and so on. This rationalist approach has influenced a number of analysts of conversation, most notably those working in a Gricean framework: their work is discussed in Chapter 5 below. The notion of rules as essentially normative is also significant for ethnomethodological conversation analysis. For an ethnomethodologist, what is crucial is not so much the rational character of everyday exchanges as the idea that such exchanges conform to a criterion of intersubjective accountability. We explore this idea further in Chapter 6.

To sum up, then, it appears that in the social scientific tradition a rule is a followable prescription which social actors employ because it is a rational means to their ends, and/or because sanctions may be attached to rule-violation. The supposition that actors are following rules accounts for behavioural regularities; but the rules approach goes beyond the mere statement of regularities because the actor is normally credited with know-ledge (overt or tacit) of the rule (in fact, researchers often have to go to great lengths, such as what Harré calls 'Garfinkeling' (manipulating behaviour and asking for comments on deviant examples which will reveal tacit knowledge of non-deviant cases) in order to present any evidence for their claims). Rules in this tradition are not like causal laws, hypotheses *about* behaviour: they are shared norms which actors use to *guide* their behaviour.

Rules of grammar

The topic of grammatical rules is a complex one which has an extensive literature of its own. For our present purposes, however, it is sufficient to point out some important respects in which rules of grammar are very different from the social scientist's rules. In the discussion that follows, we take our notion of a rule of grammar from the paradigm which has dominated debate on this issue: that is, the generative/Chomskyan paradigm. However, many other rule formulations used in linguistics (e.g. Labovian variable rules; alternation/co-occurrence rules) could equally be used to illustrate our point, since they diverge from the social scientific rule-concept in similar ways to the generative rule.

The first major divergence between the two notions of what a rule is, is that grammatical rules are not usually envisaged by generativists as follow-able prescriptions (indeed this is the basis for the argument put forward by Baker and Hacker (1984b) that rules of grammar are not really rules at all). A rule of grammar is not a social norm, nor is it the result of choice. People do not have the option of, say, violating the principle of subjacency: that principle characterizes a regularity from which non-brain-damaged speakers are unlikely to deviate. Certainly, rules of grammar may describe an idealization, linguistic competence, but the important point here is that they are conceptualized as unconscious and invariant.

Secondly, and connectedly, generativists treat grammatical rules as if they made predictions by virtue of being able to characterize strings as well or ill-formed. The predictions in question concern the acceptability of strings to native speakers of a language (however, see Baker and Hacker (1984b, p. 314) for an argument that grammaticality is entailed rather than predicted).

Thirdly, explanation is an entirely different undertaking in the case of grammatical rules. Within the Chomskyan paradigm there is a presumption of autonomy, that is the irreducibility of grammar to anything else (though in 'modular' accounts, performance reflects the interaction of grammar with other factors). Grammatical rules are not held to be relative to goals or to the functions language fulfils. The most likely explanation of a grammatical rule, then, involves postulating universal constraints on the form of natural languages, constraints which are ultimately built into the neural apparatus of the language-learner.

It is perhaps surprising that this grammatical conception of a rule has had any influence whatever on conversation analysis, yet a glance at the literature confirms that it has. Especially among analysts who favour a structural rather than pragmatic or ethnographic approach, the notion that one should formulate quasi-generative rules to account for observed distributional regularities has been widely accepted without very much reflection. Many analysts draw explicit parallels between syntactic structure and the organization of discourse: Stubbs, for example, asserts that in each case 'the basic aim is to predict the surface distribution of forms' (1981, p. 107). It is even supposed by some conversation analysts that speakers 'know' the rules of conversation in the same unconscious, involuntary way they know syntactic rules, and that the rules themselves are similarly invariant. Labov and Fanshel, for example, remark that 'the rules of discourse . . . are like the rules of syntax in their unconscious, invariant nature' (1977, p. 75). They also surmise that these rules are 'compelling'—that is, we unconsciously have to conform to them. In the work of some linguists this orientation reaches the extreme point where it is clear that their goal is nothing less than a grammar of conversation: as Edmondson (1981, p. 190) puts it:

> It should be possible to formulate a set of discourse formulation rules which would recursively enumerate an unbounded number of interactional structures.

The work of Labov and Fanshel, Edmondson and Stubbs will be discussed in Chapters 3 and 4. They are unlike the Griceans, and only partly resemble the ethnomethodologists, firstly in considering formal sequential organization to be the fundamental problem in the analysis of conversation; and secondly in regarding abstract, invariant, quasi-grammatical rules as the basis for that sequential organization (rather than some notion of a 'rational exchange' or a set of shared conventions, for example).

Problems in the concept 'conversational rule'

From the above discussion it should be evident that when we refer in this book to the concept 'conversational rule' we are not dealing with a single monolithic entity. The concept of a rule is a means of encapsulating certain regularities of conversational interaction; but analysts who make use of this device may have very different sorts of regularity in their sights (to assert that particular sequences of speech acts 'regularly' occur is different from claiming that speakers 'regularly' try to avoid giving offence, for instance) and furthermore, they may hold differing views about what it means to describe behaviour as rule-governed. For some analysts this is tantamount to saying that conversationalists are actually *following* the rules, making rational choices whose implications they can weigh up. For others, all it appears to imply is that the data of talk display certain regularities, which some formulation will describe or reproduce.

From the notion of conversational rules in general, it seems then that a number of questions arise, and we would like to pick out two in particular.

The first question concerns the difference between *rules* and *regularities*. Is it the case that *any* regularity which we discern in conversational interaction should be taken as evidence for the existence of a rule? In the social scientific paradigm mentioned above, it is clear that more than just regularities are needed to justify the writing of rules: there has to be some evidence that social actors are following a prescription (for instance, that they can refer to the relevant norm overtly; or that violations are repaired or sanctioned). What might count as evidence is an issue the ethnomethodologists have addressed in their notion that members 'orient to' rules. Yet in practice their claims are not always unproblematic, as we show in our account of CA (Chapter 6). The analysts of the 'Birmingham school', particularly Stubbs and McTear, have defended their belief that conversation is rule-governed on the grounds that speakers can make a distinction (mirroring that between grammatical and ungrammatical sentences) between 'well-formed' discourse and 'ill-formed' discourse. Yet they take it for granted that speakers can do this because they have tacit knowledge of certain conversational rules—a conclusion which is far from being logically inevitable. How far regularities are underlain by rules, and what the grounds are for saying some behaviour is rule-governed, are issues which will concern us further in this book.

The second question concerns *explanation*. We have already quoted Brown and Levinson's view that for most conversation analysts, or students of social behaviour in general, the mere formulation of a rule is enough and no further elucidation is felt to be required. A number of analysts, on the other hand, have felt a need to motivate conversational rules, and the approaches to be discussed later make suggestions about this. Their suggestions include various higher-order theoretical constructs, both linguistic (as in Clarke's notion of a native conversationalist's 'competence') and non-linguistic (goals, rationality, etc.). We need to ask how compelling these proposals are, as well as exploring the difficult issue of how conversational organization could in principle be explained. The problem alluded to by McLaughlin (1984, pp. 259–260)) remains:

> There may be innumerable rules, each subscribed to by a different set of persons, which cover the same behaviors in the identical contexts, yet

rules theorists have not provided us with any coherent accounts as to why persons choose to follow one rule rather than another.

The question which arises here in relation to current approaches to the analysis of conversation is whether a satisfactory solution to the problem— an explanation, in short, of conversationalists' behaviour—does not push the framework of micro-analysis beyond its limits.

Units

Many models of conversation, particularly those in the 'structural' category, have made use of the idea that conversational data can be broken down into its component parts or units. Furthermore, the units proposed are almost always similar in being functional rather than formal, their prototype being the single act performed in speaking.

Pike, as we have seen, invented the 'behavioreme', a unit analogous to the phoneme or the morpheme inasmuch as it is defined by contrastive function and distribution; Sinclair and Coulthard (1975) draw up a 'rankscale' or hierarchical ordering of functional units: act, move, exchange, transaction, with *move* (like a move in chess or draughts) as the fundamental discourse component. A similar hierarchical principle is operative in the ethnomethodologist's notion of an 'adjacency pair' made up of two 'pair parts'. Other analysts such as Willis Edmondson (1981) and Labov and Fanshel (1977) have made more explicit use of the illocutionary act as a basic unit. This is not altogether different from the move or behavioreme, though it gives more emphasis to intention as a determinant of function than Pike or the ethnomethodologists or Coulthard, who rely more on position in discourse.

That so many analysts are in broad agreement on what the basic units of conversation are—in contrast to their confusion and disagreement about rules—might suggest that the whole notion of the conversational unit is unproblematic. This, however, is not the case. The general concept of a unit may not be contested to the same degree as that of a rule, but the quest for plausible units of talk raises several problems. Again, we pick out a number for brief consideration here; they will arise again at various points in later chapters.

Three problems in dealing with units of talk seem to us especially significant and troublesome. They are first, the problem of *segmentation*; second, the problem of *classification*; and third, the problem of *type-token relations*. To ask what the units of conversation are is to raise the question of how to segment conversational data, while any segmentation inevitably leads to the issue of classifying or typing the segments. A satisfactory model must incorporate principled and reliable criteria for dividing data into segments, plus an exhaustive classificatory apparatus which does not leave segments unaccounted for, nor allow *ad hoc* categories to proliferate. There must also be some way of clarifying type-token relations, so that the identification of a particular segment with a general category will be reliable and unambiguous. All these requirements present difficulties in practice, as many current models of conversation show.

Take, for example, the problem of segmentation. In the absence of formal criteria for identifying a stretch of talk as one unit, it is not uncommon for the analyst to be unsure where the boundary should be drawn. Coulthard and his associates have observed, for instance, that the less interactive conversation becomes, the more it tends towards monologue, the more the analyst finds series of moves which are impossible to divide up with any real certainty. Segmentation becomes arbitrary and unilluminating.

Pike is one of the few conversation analysts to consider this problem theoretically and in detail. He believes that any illuminating analysis must be *emic*—that is to say, must reproduce the categories and principles of segmentation used by social actors themselves. Thus he can only recognize a boundary where conversationalists would also recognize one. Accordingly he introduces the criterion of 'closure': the boundaries of a behavioreme are marked by various cues which signal recognition on the part of the actor that a meaningful act has now been completed. This criterion, Pike hopes,

> allows us to stop short of the *reductio ad absurdum* of treating the movement of some particular molecule in some particular muscle of some part of the vocal organs during the production of some particular sound as constituting a behavioreme on a theoretical par with the football game (Pike, 1967, p. 130).

But Pike's emic criterion of closure or purposiveness raises the crucial problem of intersubjectivity. The criterion will only work if people actually *agree* on what is purposive and whether some stretch of behaviour comprises one meaningful act. We have already pointed out that it is open to question whether people really do share intuitions about this, whether they do in fact identify the same unit boundaries. And even supposing they do, the further question arises of how and why they do.

Exactly the same problem of intersubjectivity applies to both the classification of unit types and the identification of tokens with those types. If it is questionable whether people agree on what constitutes one unit, it is equally questionable whether they agree on the meaning or function of a piece of talk. The attempt to construct a satisfactory taxonomy of units is a feature of most versions of converation analysis, from Searle's theoretical classification of illocutionary acts (1971) to the empirical taxonomies of moves produced by researchers from the English Language Research group at Birmingham (see Coulthard and Montgomery, 1981). We will therefore be paying close attention throughout this book to the assumptions made in constructing a classificatory apparatus, as well as to the success of particular taxonomies in accommodating conversational data.

We have tried to establish that rules and units occupy an important place in the conversation analytic tradition that has developed so rapidly since 1970. Partly, the importance of rules and units can be ascribed to the general popularity among social scientists of the axiom that meaningful behaviour is rule-governed; partly, however, it is a direct result of the success of lower-level linguistic analyses which have made extensive use of taxonomies and rules to describe the regularities found in language use in terms of syntagmatic and paradigmatic relations. We have also identified a number of problems associated with the rules and units approach, especially with its extension to the analysis of conversation.

In the following chapter we embark on a series of detailed discussions in which these general observations on rules and units are developed. The particular approach to be examined in Chapter 2 is that of several influential social psychologists: Starkey Duncan, Donald Fiske and David Clarke. We begin with these social psychologists because of their insistence on controlled experimental methods, and the inductive methodology which is a feature of their work. These characteristics of social psychological conversation analysis make it peculiarly well-suited to demonstrate clearly the nature and shortcomings of the rules and units framework.

2

The Social Psychological Study of Conversation

Introduction

There can be little doubt that conversational organization is a perfect topic of study for social psychology. For where else but in conversational interaction does one find such an exemplary integration of the psychology of the individual and the sociology of the group? And is not that integration the main concern which unites disparate researchers into the field of social psychology? At the same time, conversational organization appears to be the perfect subject for an analysis using the characteristically inductive methods of social psychology. It is a relatively straightforward task to collect conversational data, and that data lends itself to statistical analysis particularly well. Should social psychology achieve a breakthrough in the mapping of conversational structure, it would boost considerably the reputation of social psychology in the disciplinary marketplace and establish its inductive/experimental methodology as foremost in the social sciences.

Consequently, it is no surprise that conversational interaction should have attracted an increasing amount of attention from social psychologists. Every aspect of verbal and nonverbal behaviour in conversation seems to have been the subject of experiments, research projects and long-term studies. A full bibliography of all these studies would in itself occupy a larger book than this one. A detailed survey would require volumes.

However, as with other models of conversation analysis studied in this book, it is not our intention to provide a comprehensive survey of social psychological research on conversation, nor to offer an introductory over-view of the methods used in that research. Rather, our aim is to demonstrate that social psychologists have produced a version of the rules and units approach, and to examine the specific ways in which they have addressed the problems of discovering conversational units and rules.

Experiments in social psychology

In this chapter the methodological framework of social psychology will be illustrated through a discussion of four important and yet quite characteristic experiments performed by social psychologists over the last fifteen years. What is characteristic about these experiments is the inductive methodology on which they are based. This in turn is related to the assumption that controlled experimentation is the discovery procedure best suited to reveal, step by step, the underlying organization of conversational interaction. Social psychologists typically have as objectives:

1. The isolation (by induction from empirical observations) of a set of acts which may reliably be identified in conversation.
2. The discovery of rules regulating the deployment of these acts in conversational interaction.

These objectives and the methods used to attain them will be discussed in relation to four experiments: two by Starkey Duncan and Donald Fiske, and two by David Clarke. We will follow our consideration of these experiments with a more general discussion of the inductive approach.

Duncan and Fiske's external-variable study

In their book *Face-to-Face Interaction* (1977), Duncan and Fiske discuss at length two quite different studies they have performed on conversational interaction. The first they call an 'external-variable study' and the second a 'structural study'. Because the external-variable study adopts the more traditional experimental approach, it is this which we will consider first.

Guiding the external-variable study was an underlying hypothesis that an analysis of the statistical correlations between the frequencies of various types of acts performed in a conversation should provide an explanatory foundation for answers to questions such as the following. Why, during a five-minute interaction, did one speaker succeed in producing consistently longer turns than the other? What was the consequence of the tendency of some speakers not to gaze at their hearer while speaking? Why, after the conversations, would some interactants be characterized by their co-conversationalists as sociable, while others were characterized as solitary? Were those characterizations linked to the way the interactants behaved in conversation?

Perhaps an analogy might help to explain the logic behind this study. Those who follow televised sports are familiar with the statistical analyses the commentators inevitably invoke as explanations for the outcome of particular matches. They will explain, for example, the whereas McEnroe only succeeded with 43% of his first serves, Lendl had a 67% success rate. At the same time, although Lendl only approached the net sixteen times, he won all but one of those points, whereas McEnroe came to the net 32 times, however only winning 50% of points played there. Or we might be told that although Lendl and McEnroe fared equally well on their backhands, with a 70% success rate, compared to 95% for both of them on their forehands, McEnroe was forced by his opponent to play twice the number of backhands that Lendl played. In the end, such statistical summaries of the individual strokes and moves made by each of the opponents will be invoked as an explanation for Lendl's convincing win over McEnroe in straight sets.

Duncan and Fiske's study used data obtained by video-taping 88 subjects conversing in pairs, making a total of seven hours of recorded conversations. The subjects, all graduate students at the University of Chicago, were taped in a controlled setting in the visible presence of the recording equipment. Only five minutes of each seven-minute interaction was subjected to detailed analysis.

Although the videotaped conversations were not given a full verbal transcription, trained transcriptionists (or 'raters') scrutinized each conversation, carefully noting every occurrence of any of a long list of types of conversational activity.

> Each action was coded by a trained rater, rating only one action for each pass of the tape. The raters were encouraged to replay segments of the tape as many times as necessary to record each kind of action or to time it accurately with a stopwatch. Each speaking turn was counted and timed, each nodding of the head was counted, each period of gesturing was counted and timed, etc. (Duncan and Fiske, 1977, p. 37).

The procedure which Duncan and Fiske call 'coding', or 'rating' (i.e. where one or more 'raters' study the videotape for instances of particular classes of communicative acts) will be discussed at length later in this chapter.

The experiment relies on the assumption that verbal behaviour consists of discrete acts. The acts chosen for study were selected for a variety of reasons. In some cases the investigators chose a particular act on the basis of intuitive 'hunches', guessing that the act chosen would prove to be significant. In other cases, previous studies suggested the potential importance of an act. All acts chosen were those which could be identified with a very high degree of replicability by the coders and which could be taught to others by ostensive definition: i.e. by means of 'pointing to a few specific instances on a videotape projection' (Duncan and Fiske, 1977, p. 37).

> Thus the definitions, implicit or explicit, were usually in physical terms. We wanted to avoid any interpretation by the coder, such as would be required to code approving looks, disparaging gestures, or nervous laughs (Duncan and Fiske, 1977, p. 37).

Consequently, the acts chosen for coding were primarily physical acts, such as laughing, smiling, pausing, turn length, nodding, gesturing, foot movement, self-grooming, etc. They avoided acts which had to be defined in terms of what they call 'unobservables'. That is, they did not include such potential conversational acts as offending, flattering, explaining, etc.: to identify instances of such acts coders would have to speculate about the speaker's intentions, the hearer's private reaction, and other such 'unobservable' states or events. The one real exception to this restriction allowed by Duncan and Fiske was that of 'social questions', defined as 'the person asking the other a question about him which naturally invites him to take a turn to answer the question' (Duncan and Fiske, 1977, p. 42). Later in this chapter we will discuss at length the distinction made by Duncan and Fiske between 'observables' and 'unobservables'.

The following is a list of the variables studied by Duncan and Fiske in their analysis of the 88 two-party interactions.

1. Turn time	26. Gaze time
2. Turn number	27. Gesture time speaking
3. Turn mean length	28. Gesture extent speaking
4. Interruption rate	29. Gesture mean length speaking
5. Filled pause rate	30. Gesture rate speaking
6. Social question number	31. Self-adaptor number
7. Nod rate	32. Self-adaptor extent speaking
8. Short vocal back-channel rate	33. Self-adaptor extent not speaking
9. Long vocal back-channel rate	34. Self-adaptor time
10. All back-channel rate	35. Self-adaptor mean length speaking
11. Smile number	36. Self-adaptor mean length not speaking
12. Smile extent speaking	37. Self-adaptor mean lengh
13. Smile extent not speaking	38. Foot movement time
14. Smile time	39. Foot movement number
15. Laugh rate speaking	40. Foot movement mean length
16. Laugh rate not speaking	41. Seat (shifts seat) rate speaking
17. Laugh number	42. Seat rate not speaking
18. Gaze (at partner) number	43. Seat number
19. Gaze rate speaking	44. Leg (shifts leg) rate speaking
20. Gaze rate not speaking	45. Leg rate not speaking
21. Gaze mean length speaking	46. Leg number
22. Gaze mean length not speaking	47. Shift (seat of leg) rate speaking
23. Gaze mean length	48. Shift rate not speaking
24. Gaze extent speaking	49. Shift number
25. Gaze extent not speaking	(Duncan and Fiske, 1977, pp. 42–45).

The main thing to be noticed about these variables (and this is what, within conversation analysis, is distinctive about the external-variable study) is that individual acts, such as a movement of the foot, a smile, or a hand gesture, are totalled over time for each individual interaction. That is, they are not treated as independently significant acts. An analogous study of the dialogues at a phonetic level might include variables such as total time producing nasal vowels, number of stop consonants, mean length of fricatives, etc. Obviously, this would be an extraordinary approach to the study of phonetic acts. Nevertheless, such an approach is characteristic of the study of animal behaviour as well as of the traditional psychological study of human non-verbal communication.

Having obtained scores for each of the variables listed, these scores were then statistically analysed for significant correlations. So, for example, turn time was found to have positive correlations with the rate of gaze when not speaking. That is, there was found to be a predictable relationship between the amount of time a speaker held the floor and the frequency with which their hearer brought their gaze to the speaker. On the other hand, turn time was found not to have positive correlations with the frequency with which the speaker brought their gaze to the hearer. Such relations were further complicated by noting their variation with respect to the sex of the speaker, the sex of the hearer, and to whether the interaction studied was the first or second in which the subjects were participating.

In the second part of their experiment Duncan and Fiske attempted to discover if any significant correlations existed between the scores obtained on the act variables and the participants' descriptions of their personalities.

> It seemed reasonable to expect that a person's personality would be related to his behaviour, in this case, his acts in an interpersonal situation (Duncan and Fiske, 1977, p. 99).

Personality self-descriptions were obtained before the interactions by asking each participant to fill out a battery of special tests. These included, for instance, one form including 300 descriptive adjectives which the subject was asked to check if they applied to his/her own personality. Subsequently, a statistical study was made of the correlations between the adjectives checked and the scores obtained the act variables.

The results obtained in both parts of the study were disappointing.

> Our substantive findings from our studies of correlates of acts in interaction do not impress us. While the number of observed relation-ships was large, it formed a small proportion of the total number of correlations computed. In other words, the proportion of large correlations was not greatly above the proportion which would be expected by chance (Duncan and Fiske, 1977, p. 123).

In their discussion of the external-variable study, Duncan and Fiske consider the reasons for its failure to produce significant results. The most revealing conclusion they draw is that, in effect, the external-variable approach, by summarizing scores, overlooks the detailed, moment-by-moment way in which acts relate to other acts. Their original research topic took the following form:

> . . . with what other acts is this act correlated, when scores are obtained for each act over the entire five minutes that were coded? (Duncan and Fiske, 1977, pp. 130–131).

And yet they conclude that the act scores, summarized for particular types of act over a five-minute interaction, did not appear to have statistically significant relationships between them. Instead, they speculate, it is possible that a procedure such as that followed in this study is incapable of grasping the significant relationships which individual acts have to other individual acts (either by the same or different actors), and that it misses those relationships precisely because of its quantitative procedure of counting, totalling, and averaging act occurrences, regardless of the individual circumstances in which the acts occurred.

> Our basic datum unit was a score obtained by summing acts over an entire period (. . .). We sought to determine whether such total scores covaried over persons, keeping constant the total situation and, in the subanalyses, the sex of the person and other variables (. . .) What unity does such a series of acts have? Without realizing it, we used this scoring practice to indicate some general disposition of the participant for displaying the act, under favourable circumstances for eliciting it. But what are these circumstances? We are unable to answer that question from our correlational data (Duncan and Fiske, 1977, p. 131).

In other words, Duncan and Fiske came to the realization that acts, or the relationships between acts, cannot be added together to produce a quantitative sum which is in any way revealing about the role of those acts in the interactions studied. The upshot of their discussion is that Duncan and Fiske rejected the external variable approach as a means for discovering the structure of conversational interaction. It is perhaps surprising that they ever supposed it would succeed.

It is worth considering a general lesson that can be learned from the failure of the external-variable study. Although generality and context-independence are usually regarded as positive qualities of scientific explanation, in the case of conversation analysis this may not always be true. For as the failure of Duncan and Fiske's study shows, the further away the analysis gets from the specific and situated characteristics of conversational acts, the more distorted becomes the understanding of the original function of those acts. In the case of the external-variable study, the distortion brought on by the quantitative, generalizing techniques is so great that the results obtained lack any significance.

David Clarke's 'test frame' and 'stochastic' studies

Still within the social psychological tradition, a different approach to conversation analysis is that developed by David Clarke at Oxford University. Like Duncan and Fiske, Clarke's research may be divided into two distinct stages. While the first of these stages shares Duncan and Fiske's inductive approach, the second abandons it in favour of the hypothetico-deductive model popularized by generative linguistics. Since this second stage is quite similar to the linguistic studies of conversation which we will be discussing in later chapters, our focus here will be on Clarke's earlier inductively-oriented experiments.

In spite of a shared inductive methodology, Clarke's experiments differ greatly from Duncan and Fiske's external-variable study. Firstly, there is a difference in the units chosen as basic elements of the sought after conversational organization. Duncan and Fiske had restricted their study to that of observable, physical actions. Clarke, on the other hand, comes to take the speech act as the structural unit of conversation. As a result of this difference, the studies of Clarke and of Duncan and Fiske appear quite dissimilar. This superficial appearance is reinforced by the second major difference in their methodologies. While Duncan and Fiske's external-variable study follows a traditional experimental design, inherited from the psychological study of non-verbal communication and from ethology, Clarke borrows his experimental design from structural linguistics, especially from the methods used by the American distributionalists of the 1940s and 1950s. Finally, Clarke advocates an 'emic' perspective, according to which the subject's perception is employed to assist in unitizing, categorizing, and analysing the structure of the flow of behaviour. Largely because of their focus on physical acts, Duncan and Fiske adopt an 'etic' perspective, in which analytical decisions are ideally made as objective as possible.

In addition to differences in their experimental methodologies, Clarke's studies differ from the external-variable study in their goals. The aims of those of Clarke's experiments which we will look at here are to locate the level(s) at which conversational organization operates and to discover categories of conversational acts and the sequential relations between them. Thus, Clarke's approach does not make the same mistake as that which vitiates the external-variable study: viz. that of treating individual acts as quantifiable parts of an overall sum. Instead, the key to Clarke's approach is first to look for the substitutional (paradigmatic) and combinational (syntagmatic) properties of individual acts and then, on the basis of these properties, to establish hierarchical classes of act-types.

In the first experiment discussed in his book *Language and Action: A Structural Model of Behaviour* (Clarke, 1983) Clarke took transcriptions of conversations recorded between subjects at the Oxford laboratories and wrote down each utterance on an individual 4×6 inch file card, 'bearing no other information as to the original speaker or the nature of the sequence, which later subjects could use' (Clarke, 1983, p. 46). He then presented these cards, randomly re-ordered, to a second set of subjects and asked them to arrange the order of the utterances into what they assumed to be the original order of their production. Clarke summarizes the results as follows:

Subjects were able to reassemble the conversations with greater than chance accuracy, reaching significance levels of 10^{-10} and 10^{-11} on a few items. This suggests that the original dialogues did embody some systematic relationship between verbal context and the nature of each utterance (and) that the pattern is one on which the native speaker can pass judgement from his own knowledge of the speech community . . . (Clarke, 1983, p. 49).

Having come to the conclusion that conversation has a sequential pattern, Clarke proceeds in the two subsequent experiments to investigate the level at which that pattern operates, or, more precisely, to discover the nature of the cues which allow the subjects to attain considerable success in retrieving an original pattern. In the second experiment Clarke devises a test similar to the first experiment, but with an original dialogue, not generated in the same fashion as the first, but rather produced by subjects writing alternate lines of a hypothetical dialogue. In addition, 'they were asked to use complete, well-formed sentences as far as possible, but avoiding third person pronouns, all articles, and all relative clauses' (Clarke, 1983, p. 52). At the same time

Each utterance had to be a statement or a question in the present tense and active voice, and had to be comprehensible in itself without reference to other utterances in the dialogue (Clarke, 1983, p. 52).

The point of this extremely artificial technique of dialogue generation was to eliminate all syntactic clues which might have helped the first set of subjects determine the original order in which the utterances were produced. Again the experiment was deemed a success:

The great reduction in syntactic variation brought about by the grammatical constraints used in this experiment did not result in any reduction in the subjects' performance. (. . .) the ability to recognize sequential structure in dialogue does not seem to depend on syntactic information alone. There must be other properties of the utterances which vary systematically with verbal context (Clarke, 1983, pp. 53–54).

In the third experiment Clarke attempted to determine whether the knowledge which allowed subjects to retrieve the original sequences was based on semantic or pragmatic factors. On the hunch that pragmatic knowledge was the determining factor, he devised an experiment which dispensed with the stage of dialogue generation and instead made use of the findings of Bales's 1953 study on the frequencies of different event sequences. In this study Bales had coded each utterance of a conversational corpus as an instance of a particular type of event category (not significantly dissimilar, for present purposes, from the speech act categories Clarke later comes to adopt). He then studied the probabilities of particular sequences of events, coming up with a transitional probability matrix of reactive tendencies. Clarke then made use of Bales's findings as a control for his own experiment in which, given only a brief description of each of Bales's twelve event categories, subjects were asked to determine the likelihood that an instance of a given event-category would be followed by an instance of any of the other eleven categories. (That is, for category 1 they were to decide which of the remaining eleven categories would be the most probable *sequitur*, which would be the next most likely, and so on.) The results obtained were then compared with Bales's data. Although the comparison did not produce strongly positive results, Clarke found nevertheless that they supported his hypothesis that it is event-types, rather than syntactic or semantic units, which serve as the basic units in the sequential organization of conversational interaction (Clarke, 1983, pp. 60–61).

Thus, the first stage of Clarke's study of conversation led him to the conclusions that conversations do possess a sequential structure, that conversational participants know which sequences are probable and which are not, and that the units so structured are neither syntactic nor semantic in nature, but rather are pragmatic events, similar to the speech acts first identified by J. L. Austin. These conclusions in turn led him to the methodological hypothesis that the best way to identify the structure of conversation would be to adopt the methods developed in structural linguistics for the analysis of grammatical structure.

> . . . the rules which will generate all and only the speech-act sequences which are sensible conversations are so like the rules which will generate all and only the morpheme strings which are well-formed sentences, that the study of the former may be assisted by the techniques for investigating the latter (Clarke, 1983, p. 106).

Following the linguistic analogy, Clarke postulates three stages in the analysis of speech act sequences: unitization, categorization and sequential analysis. The stage of unitization consists in the segmentation of the conversational flow, or 'stream of behaviour', into discrete chunks suitable for further analysis. Clarke does not recommend the development of a special unitizing procedure but assumes that segmentation into speech act units is intuitive and straightforward (Clarke, 1983, p. 137). Instead, where the major problems arise is in the second stage of categorization. Here, the units segmented in the first stage are to be classified into various types. Clarke argues that, like the categorization of linguistic units such as the morpheme, the categorization of speech acts must integrate paradigmatic (substitutional) and syntagmatic (combinational) considerations. He hypothesizes that the question whether a stretch of behaviour functions as an instance of a given act category requires an answer which considers the context in which the behaviour is occurring. In one context, the verbal sequence 'What are you doing tonight?' will be interpreted as a request for information (e.g. a mother asking her son about his homework schedule), but in another context that same verbal sequence will be interpreted as 'making a pass' (e.g. a solitary man addressing a solitary woman in a 'singles' bar). Consequently, categorization cannot fail to pay attention to syntagmatic considerations, i.e. to the contexts in which the event being classified is taking place.

Acting on this hypothesis, Clarke devised an experiment which was intended to reveal basic categories of speech acts, much as 'test-frame analysis' in linguistics is designed to reveal morpheme categories, or what are traditionally called 'parts of speech'. The first part of this experiment consisted in asking twenty subjects to write a realistic dialogue of forty lines. They were told to make sure

> . . . to keep the two speakers 'in register' so that every odd-numbered (line), counting from the top of the page, would contain an utterance by speaker X, and every even-numbered (line) an utterance by speaker Y. This hypothetical, but well-formed dialogue invented by each subject was to function as the test frame in the next part of the experiment. In producing the dialogues subjects were asked to bear in mind the diversity of roles and settings which can contribute to dyadic encounters, and to try between them to encompass a variety of normal dialogue types. They were told that each utterance or line of dialogue should consist of one 'move' and only one move (i.e. move=speech act). The implications of this instruction were explained to the subjects (Clarke, 1983, p. 149).

In the second part of the experiment the subjects were instructed to take the middle twenty lines of the dialogue they had written and to suggest four plausible substitutions for each line. They were told to select substitutes which, if inserted for the original in the dialogue itself, 'would produce another well-formed and meaningful dialogue, although its meaning need not be that of the original' (Clarke, 1983, p. 149). Again, the subjects were told to ensure that each substitute line consisted of only one 'move' or speech act.

Thus, this experiment reproduces the format of test-frame analysis, in which morpheme categories are established by determining which morphemes can be substituted for which others in various contextual slots. So 'boy', 'dog' and 'table' would all be classified as nouns because they could be substituted as variables in 'She saw the ——.' And 'liked', 'examined' and 'sold' would be classified as verbs because they could be substituted for 'saw' in the same test-frame. It should be noted that test-frame analysis relies on the possibility of clearly distinguishing well-formed strings (or dialogues) from ill-formed ones, for this is the criterion on which the substitutability of an element is determined. If, in substituting 'a' for 'b' in the well-formed sequence 'XbY', a non-well-formed sequence results, then 'a' and 'b' cannot be taxonomically classified in the same category. Clarke never discusses the possibility of distinguishing well-formed from ill-formed dialogues, nor does he reveal how it was determined which of the dialogues the subjects produced in the first part of this experiment were well-formed. (We will discuss this topic more fully in Chapter 4.)

The third part of the experiment involved a second set of subjects sorting each of the groups of proposed substitutes, produced by the first set of subjects, into piles of 'functional equivalents' (Clarke, 1983, p. 150). The aim here was to reduce the original 374 groups of substitute acts, resulting from the first two parts of the experiment, into a smaller set of act categories, hoping thereby to discover 'a true partition of the set of speech-acts' (Clarke, 1983, p. 150). The sortings produced by this process were then subjected to a single-linkage cluster analysis in order to reveal the degree to which this second set of subjects agreed on particular classifications.

It is important to note that this third part of the experiment is a departure from the use of test-frame analysis in linguistics. If it worked properly, the test-frame experiment on morpheme classification would result in a clear division of the morphemes into a finite set of categories. No third part of the analysis would be required, i.e. a part in which subjects took the results of the groupings produced in the first two parts and then sorted these into still smaller groups. Indeed, such a step would constitute an abandonment of the test-frame procedure, for the second set of subjects are not producing groups of equivalents using mutual-substitutability as the crucial criterion. Instead, in the Clarke experiment, the criterion they are told to follow is one of 'functional equivalence'. This amounts to asking the subjects to put two sub-groups of acts into the same pile if they 'do the same thing'. By thus resorting to intuitive judgement in order to determine equivalence, Clarke abandons the controlled procedure of the test-frame.

In commenting on the results of this complex experiment, Clarke admits that, as an attempt to reveal classes of speech acts, the experiment was a failure. No clear classes were produced by the cluster analysis. That is to say, of the 374 groups of five acts which, in the third part of the experiment, the 12 subjects were to sort into smaller groups, no clear pattern of sorting emerged. Consequently, no clear taxonomy of speech act categories emerged from the experiment.

Faced with the failure of his inductively-based attempt to identify categories of speech acts, Clarke decided to abandon the inductive approach to categorization, because '. . . the categories cannot be derived from a simple test-frame procedure' (Clarke, 1983, p. 157). In subsequent experiments he employs an *a priori* list of categories, drawn in large part from the English vocabularly of speech-act terms (e.g. 'threat', 'promise', 'offend', 'blame', 'boast', etc.) (Clarke, 1983, p. 159).

The most notable of the subsequent experiments is the 'stochastic' study (Clarke, 1983, pp. 162–168). The point of this experiment was to identify statistically regular sequences of speech acts. A similar study in linguistics would be based on a statistical study of the most common sequences of two (or more) words; the results of this study could then be said to indicate the class of probable sentences. So, if it were found that articles were most commonly followed by nouns, nouns by verbs and verbs by adjectives, a common sentence combination would be article-noun-verb-adjective (e.g. *The boy looked tired*).

It is important to note the fundamental contrast between such a study of chains of transition probabilities and the previous test-frame study. In the latter, all that is tested is, for instance, whether 'looked' can *possibly* ever follow 'the boy', not whether it is a *probable* occurrence.

Clarke describes the experimental format for this study as follows.

> Thirty-three subjects from the subject panel of the Oxford University Department of Experimental Psychology came into the laboratory and were given (a) list of utterance categories and definitions. . . . They were also told to use the symbol # like an 'event' to mark the boundary between two topics and # # to mark the boundary between two different dialogues. Each subject then received a response sheet marked out into 100 consecutive boxes, each containing a space to write A or B to differentiate the identities of two 'speakers', and a space to write one of the utterance types. Subjects were asked to produce 100 lines of hypothetical dialogue using this notation of A's and B's for speakers, the speech-act types for their utterances, and the additional punctuating symbols for the boundaries of topics, or whole conversations (Clarke, 1983, pp. 162–163).

In order to uncover regular sequences of speech-act types in these artificial dialogues, Clarke determined the transitional frequency relations for each of the reactive (A-B) and proactive (A-A) pairs of speech-acts and, on the basis of the resultant matrix determined (using χ^2) a statistical value for each relation. The sequential pairs which were thus identified as most commonly related were then combined to form a network model of possible conversational sequences, with sequential 'chains' of up to 19 acts. For example, the following was identified as one such possible chain of acts in a conversation:

Greet+Greet+Question+Answer+Continue+Attend+Assert+
Agree.

Duncan and Fiske's 'structural' study

Before discussing this experiment critically it is best to return to consider the second major study performed by Duncan and Fiske, the 'structural' study. This study starts from the assumption that conversational interaction is rule-governed and that the rules regulate relationships between individual acts (as opposed to act-totals, as in the external-variable study). Furthermore, it is hypothesized that the rules governing a particular act and its relations may be discovered by determining which other acts it may precede or follow, which acts it may co-occur with, which acts it cannot follow, precede, or co-occur with, and which acts are possible substitutes for it. That is, in words which greatly resemble Clarke's description of his interest in the unitization and categorization of conversational acts and in their syntagmatic and paradigmatic relations, Duncan and Fiske describe the central task of 'structural' analysis as

> that of discovering and documenting the action-based elements (to be termed 'signals', 'moves', and 'units' of interaction . . .') of the organization and to specify the relationship obtaining between these elements (Duncan and Fiske, 1977, p. 138). The search for action-based elements (for example, signals) and their combinatorial relations (rules) was a primary objective . . . (Duncan and Fiske, 1977, p. 139).

In addition to sharing a similar goal with Clarke's test-frame and stochastic experiments, Duncan and Fiske's structural study adopts the same methodological assumptions as those of the latter experiment: assumption that by studying the regular sequential patterns of acts occurring in conversation, the investigator will be able to infer the rules regulating their production. Furthermore, there is the shared assumption that statistical methods are best suited for the discovery of these rule-governed regularities:

> The underlying conception of the research was that a given organization in face-to-face interaction would introduce marked regularities into the actions subject to that organization. If such were the case, then why not evaluate the proposed regularities by appropriate statistical tests? (Duncan and Fiske, 1977, p. 142).

Data for their structural study was obtained by video-taping intake interviews at the University of Chicago Counseling and Psychotherapy Research Center. The interactions took place between a therapist and applicants to the Center, both of whom were aware of being videotaped. Four new interactions were studied in addition to four of the interactions used for the external-variable study.

The first two interactions, as part of the exploratory stage of the study, were transcribed in great detail, including not only prosodic and paralinguistic features, but also a variety of features of turn length, gesture, body movement, facial expression and posture. The transcription was compiled by two transcriptionists working together on the videotape. Both transcriptionists had to agree on the transcription to be given of any given action. The nature of the 'recognition rules' used to identify instances of a particular type of action will be discussed later in this chapter. For the moment, it is sufficient to note that, as in Clarke's stochastic study, it was simply taken for granted that conversational interaction consists of discrete tokens of repeatable act-types and that the adequacy of the categorization system used will be reflected in the amount of agreement in the transcriptionists' results.

Obviously, given such a detailed transcription of conversational activity, both verbal and non-verbal, there is a high probability of finding regularly patterned relationships between types of acts. In order to reduce the size of their research task, Duncan and Fiske decided to restrict the focus of the subsequent stages of the study to the occurrence of one regular and important conversational event: the exchange of speaking turns. Their aim became the study of regularities in the acts preceding and following turn-exchange in order that they might discover the rule-governed system by which they hypothesized that exchange is routinely managed.

> The research issue would be framed in the following way: to what extent is it possible to find regularities in the transcription that (a) account for the occurrence of smooth exchanges of the speaking turn; and (b) differentiate occasions of smooth exchanges from those of simultaneous talking? (Duncan and Fiske, 1977, p. 175).

The result of their statistical analysis of the probabilities of the occurrence of particular acts before or after turn-exchange led Duncan and Fiske to the postulation of a 'turn-system' (Duncan and Fiske, 1977, pp. 176ff.) governing the exchange of speaking turns in conversation. This hypothetical turn-system itself, an intricate organization relating participant states, interaction states, 'transition readiness', actions, cues, moves and signals, is too complex to explain here. And, in any case, it is not the specifics of their system which interest us, but rather the methodological assumptions and analytical procedures which were used to 'discover' that system.

Given our purpose, then, it is only necessary that we note that, although Duncan and Fiske believe themselves to have discovered the rule-system governing turn-exchange, they confess that the patterned regularities of relations between acts on which the 'discovery' of that system was based are not perfect; they are only more or less probable.

> Despite the general strength of the regularities observed, the results were not perfect for any signal (Duncan and Fiske, 1977, p. 233).

To the obvious objection that a rule-governed system should not result in probability of occurrence of the acts so governed, but rather in perfect regularity, Duncan and Fiske respond with a variety of defensive strategies. They argue, for instance, that when a particular sequence of actions does not conform to the predicted rule-governed pattern, it may be that the actor is committing a 'performance error', i.e. is simply making an unintentional mistake. Or it may be that some of the rules are optional rather than obligatory. This would help account for the lack of perfection in the regularities. Another possibility raised is that the actors are simply violating the rule in the instance observed. A basic distinction between natural laws and rules is that the latter can be violated, although sanctions or even punishment might be the consequence. Natural laws, on the other hand, operate without exception and allow those who are subject to them no choice between obedience and violation. The rule regulating the movement of the knight in chess may be violated, i.e. it is possible for such a violation to occur. The law of gravity, however, is impossible to violate. A further explanation for the lack of perfection in the regularities, Duncan and Fiske note, is that there may be competing rules, as yet imperfectly understood by investigators. One or more of these may overrule the rule in question in certain circumstances, thus leading to imperfect patterns of regularity in the observance of that rule.

> There is no reason to view the turn system as the only such rule system applying to conversation. It seems reasonable to expect that there are a relatively large number of such rule systems, perhaps interrelated, each one applying to some distinctive aspect of conversational conduct. And, given our limited knowledge of the larger picture, it seems imperialistic to attempt to place the turn system at the center of the conversational microcosmos. Thus, a more fundamental evaluation of turn-system violations awaits development of further empirically based understanding of other aspects of conversational etiquette (Duncan and Fiske, 1977, p. 235).

With arguments such as these, Duncan and Fiske are able to defend themselves against the accusation that the merely probable regularities identified in their statistical tests admit of too many exceptions to be the products of a system of rules. And it is thus these strategies which allow them to defend the inductive experimentalist method according to which, through the observation of actual behaviour, a system of rules is hypothesized as the governing source of that behaviour. For without the benefit of such strategies the natural irregularity of human behaviour would forever frustrate the inductive 'discovery' of underlying organization.

It is in response to this very frustration that, following his own inductively-oriented 'stochastic' study, Clarke openly abandons the inductive approach to conversation analysis in favour of the hypothetico-deductive approach inspired by generative linguistic theory. For Clarke comes to the conclusion that the only regularities that the inductivist approach can unquestionably 'discover' are those that are the most trivial and obvious, and that, when more ambitious 'discoveries' are sought, the irregularity of conversational performance will continually frustrate the inductive discovery procedures. Although this is not a conclusion which Duncan and Fiske accept, thanks to their strategic 'apologies' for the gap between imperfect regularities observed and the predicted systematic regularities, it is worth citing Clarke's confession in full as a significant acknowledgement of the inductivist dilemma in conversation studies.

> The problem is this. A corpus of data has to be scanned for certain regularities which will be recorded, at the expense of others which will be ignored. The only real criterion for this, when it is done quantitatively and mechanically, is frequency of occurrence. In a commonplace phenomenon like desultory conversation the most frequently occurring regularities may seem the most banal to 'discover', and they need in no sense be more important than those discarded for being infrequent (Clarke, 1983, p. 168).

Discussion

It is now time to turn from the description of representative studies in the social psychological approach to conversation analysis to a more focused examination of the characteristically inductive and experimentalist methodology adopted in conversation analysis by social psychologists. The methodological issues we will here consider are those which form the underlying concerns of this book, viz. the problem of identifying (both categorizing types and recognizing tokens of those types) units of conversation organization and the problem of specifying the rules regulating the combination of those units. Both Duncan and Fiske as well as Clarke take these to be among the fundamental problems of conversational study. Clarke adds to these the problem of unitization: i.e. the segmentation of the behavioural stream into units capable of categorization. Duncan and Fiske, on the other hand, include both unitization and categorization under their notion of 'discovering' the elements of conversational interaction. This is understandable given that to discover the elements in the behavioral stream you have both to divide the stream into segments and to classify together those segments which are tokens of the same element-type. At the same time, Duncan and Fiske maintain a clear distinction between the initial stage in which different conversational phenomena are *categorized* as tokens of the same type and the later stage of 'coding' when, armed with a list of possible types, 'coders' (or 'raters') examine a corpus of conversations in order to *recognize* actual tokens of those categorial types. Nevertheless, both categorization and recognition instantiate the same fundamental problem: that of identifying two phenomena as the same, i.e. as members of the same class of units.

A major difference between Duncan and Fiske and Clarke on the problem of identification is that Duncan and Fiske recommend, and follow where possible, an 'etic' approach to identification while Clarke supports an 'emic' perspective. We have already alluded (Chapter 1) to this distinction, which derives from the linguistic study of speech sounds; and it is a distinction between their phonetic and phonemic descriptions. A phonemic study of speech sound only recognizes those similarities and differences in sound that are recognized and utilized by the speakers of the language concerned. A phonetic study, on the other hand, notes all detectable features of the sound, regardless of whether they are relevant to the native speaker's identification of the sounds as same or different. In principle this means that two phonetically (objectively) distinct sounds may be treated as phonemically (subjectively) identical if the substitution of one for the other in any verbal context does not result in a change of meaning. So, from a phonemic perspective a low pitch 'a' will, by English speakers, be identified as the same sound as a phonetically distinct high pitch 'a', because the substitution of one for the other (e.g. in the context 'b-th') will not change the meaning of the word. However, the substitution of an 'o' for an 'a', regardless of pitch, will change the meaning: cf. 'bath' vs. 'both'. Consequently, the phonetic difference between 'o' and 'a' is matched in English by a phonemic difference.

The transposition of this distinction to the problem of identifying units of conversational behaviour results in an opposition between an 'etic' approach, aiming for as explicit and objective procedures of identification as possible, and an 'emic' approach which relies on the intuitions of native conversationalists to identify two instances of the same conversation unit. This might mean that two stretches of conversational behaviour which are physically quite dissimilar, e.g. a nod of the head and a pronunciation of the word 'yes', and which from an 'etic' perspective would thus have to be treated as distinct entities, could from an 'emic' perspective be deemed instances of the same act: the act of assent. On the other hand, it could result in two physically identical acts being identified from an 'emic' point of view as instances of two different behavioural units. (Consider an identical utterance of 'You're crazy!', which in the context of an argument might be taken as an instance of an insult but when addressed to a comedian, in the context of a comical performance of a joke, might be taken as a compliment.)

Duncan and Fiske support an 'etic' approach to criteria of identification, asserting that maximally explicit 'recognition rules' should be used whenever possible and that 'the logical goal' of identification in the procedures of data generation.

is the entirely automatic processing of audible and visible recordings by machines, so that the data are 'untouched by human hands' (Duncan and Fiske, 1977, p. 23).

This is obviously very far from a subject-oriented 'emic' approach to identification, such as that recommended by Clarke.

> . . . there are two overwhelming reasons for choosing emically based methods. First is the need to discriminate between items of behavior lying inside and outside the system. This distinction rests on criteria of propriety and well-formedness which are only available from the native actor, who has (potential) knowledge of the rules. Secondly, the system has to be analysed in terms of its sub-components, and these are defined by the discontinuities of meaning among the population of elements, not by discontinuities in the distribution of their observable physical properties (Clarke, 1983, p. 19).

Perhaps the best way of sorting out the relative merits of these two positions and of revealing the complexity of the dilemma they are designed (but fail) to resolve is to focus our attention on the opposition between what Duncan and Fiske call 'explicit recognition rules' and 'implicit recognition rules' used by transcriptionists (or 'raters') in identifying instances of particular behavioural actions. Explicit recognition rules, in their ideal form, are tools of a strictly 'etic' methodology while implicit recognition rules incorporate the use of native intuitions characteristic of an 'emic' approach.

Fully explicit recognition rules are said by Duncan and Fiske to be exemplified in the work of Jaffe and Feldstein (1970) on turn-taking in conversation. They use automatic speech-processing equipment to identify, in an audio tape, the occurrence of speech, of simultaneous speech, and of turn-exchange. Here then, the identification of the conversational units of 'speech', 'simultaneous speech', etc., is carried out by a machine and so can be expected to be ideally objective and consistent. However, Duncan and Fiske admit that in many cases of conversation study the use of non-explicit recognition rules will be unavoidable. In this case, implicit recognition rules, exemplified by the ostensive definition of a unit ('There, that's a head-nod') are permitted. It is not made clear exactly what in the *describienda* makes it an illustration of a 'head-nod', but it is assumed that the term used, 'head-nod', already makes sense to the raters for whom the unit is being defined.

> Although fully explicit recognition rules are a goal for social science, use of implicit rules is not necessarily a major obstacle for the achievement of interjudge reliability. (. . .) This agreement is probably found because (the) classifications approximate those provided by the culture

of the raters and thus are used by them regularly, though not necessarily explicitly, in everyday life. (. . .) Thus, the investigator may successfully use implicit recognition rules for defining categories within his classification system to the extent that those categories exist in the culture of the raters. It may be added that the research will be successful only to the extent to which the categories match those existing in the culture of the observed interactants (Duncan and Fiske, 1977, pp. 15–16).

Although Duncan and Fiske approve, to some extent at least, of the use of implicit recognition rules, providing that the categories are those of the culture shared by the raters and the observed interactants, they strongly disapprove of the use of recognition rules involving reference to what they call 'unobservables'.

But there is a serious error to be avoided in developing relatively natural classification systems for studying interaction. This error occurs when the definition of the recognition rules involves the use of some supposed 'meaning' of the act, or some other unobservable entity such as intention, motivation, or the like. (. . .) It may very well happen that two raters agree entirely on the tape of action they have observed, while sharply disagreeing in their respective interpretations either of its 'meaning' in the stream of interaction, or of the intentions of the participant. (. . .) It would seem that better understanding of the impact of various actions on the stream of interaction is the object of investigation, to be approached through careful analysis of data. It is not a task assigned to a rater (Duncan and Fiske, 1977, p. 17).

In sum, Duncan and Fiske make a three-way distinction between types of recognition rules: explicit rules, implicit rules involving no unobservables, implicit rules involving unobservables. Only the first two are recommended for use in conversation analysis. However, it is neither so easy as Duncan and Fiske apparently assume to distinguish between these three types of recognition rules nor at all clear what their use in the process of identification actually provides.

Consider, for example, the ideal instantiation of an explicit recognition rule: e.g. Jaffe and Feldstein's mechanical device for the identification of speech, non-speech (i.e. pause), simultaneous speech, and turn-exchange. Such a machine, however, would identify as speech the noise produced by one of the interactants when clearing their throat or coughing. It would do so because its mechanical criterion for detecting the occurrence of speech would register as speech any vocally produced sound. Yet the clearing of one's throat would not normally be deemed as an instance of speech by any ordinary conversationalist observing the interaction in person or on tape (although it might be deemed to be an instance of speech in some contexts, by some observers). Although one might possibly be able to alter the machine so that it did not identify throat-clearing as speech (thereby creating a problem for those occasions when some conversationalists *would* identify it as speech), the general point remains the same: explicit recognition rules can be useful in identifying the occurrence of phenomena, but it is far from clear exactly what they identify the occurrence of. It is certainly not the phenomena whose occurrence is of importance to those participating in conversations. (Does the Coke machine identify the occurrence of a 'request for a drink'? Can water identify the occurrence of a 'command to boil'?) It would be more appropriate to label the phenomena which explicit recognition rules identify with invented names or numbers to make it clear that the one thing they do not identify are the types of phenomena we ordinarily refer to by such terms as 'pause', 'speech', 'interruption', 'hesitation', etc. On the other hand, it might be more accurate to refrain from using expressions such as 'recognize the occurrence of' and 'identify an instance of' in describing what it is that a mechanical explicit recognition rule does.

At the same time, as regards implicit recognition rules, Duncan and Fiske seem not to realize that there is no simple distinction to be drawn between an implicit recognition rule involving only the use of observables and an implicit rule using unobservables. They state that implicit recognition rules would be explained by ostensive definition. Thus, the analyst might produce, as a recognition rule for the conversational unit 'head-nod', an example of videotaped speech and say 'There, that's a head-nod.' It is assumed that the category 'head-nod' is part of the culture shared by the rater and the interactants observed. And presumably, the term itself makes sense to the rater because he/she is a native speaker of the language in which the expression 'head-nod' occurs, the same language used by the interactants. Thus, the notion of an implicit recognition rule implies that in order to get someone (e.g. a trainee rater) to recognize further instances of the relevant category it is sufficient to show them 'the kind of thing' that is referred to by the term and to count on the shared culture and shared language to do the rest. Consequently, it would be improper to ask English-speaking raters to find instances of 'alphas' because the term 'alpha' does not refer in English to a cultural category: 'alpha' does not stand for a behavioural category either in the raters' cultural classification system or in that of the observed conversationalists. Instead, it is an artificial category invented by the researcher, whereas the categories of 'smile', 'gesture', and 'head-nod' are part of the English cultural system. Presumably, this would continue to apply even if 'alpha' were given an ostensive definition: the prospective rater is shown a videotape in which three instances of 'alphas' occur, with the researcher pointing at each one and exclaiming 'There, that's an alpha.'

There is a problem here raised which Duncan and Fiske fail to consider, and it is a problem which confounds their attempt to make a distinction between legitimate and illegitimate use of implicit recognition rules. If the use of 'unobservables' is prohibited in recognition rules, how is one to decide if an implicit recognition rule for the identification of smiles, of head-nods, or of questions does or does not involve unobservables? For instance, Duncan and Fiske cite with approval Boomer and Dittman's (1962) study in which raters used implicit recognition rules to identify, on the one hand, 'junction pauses' and, on the other, 'hesitation pauses'. This implicit recognition rule is invoked by Duncan and Fiske as proof that unobservables need not be used. Instead, the

> subjects' implicit rule differentiating juncture from hesitation pauses presumably involved the observable elements of duration and location with respect to structural units of intonation, these units being ident-ifiable on the basis of phonological parameters (Duncan and Fiske, 1977, p. 17).

And yet, whether in fact this is what Boomer and Dittman's subjects did in *applying* the relevant implicit rule is not a question which can be decided on the basis of observables. They may, for instance, have been looking for pauses which they felt were attributable to speaker hesitation, a procedure which Duncan and Fiske would have to condemn for its reliance on unobservables. What this amounts to saying is that it is itself unobservable whether raters are employing only observables in their application of implicit recognition rules. How could we tell whether our trained raters were relying simply on observable facial movement in identifying instances of 'smiles'? Is it not unobservable whether, in the application of that rule, they are consulting their intuitions regarding the conversational context, the meaning being conveyed, the state of mind of the interactant, etc.?

It is unjustified to assume that ostensive definition will ensure that, in seeking out further examples of the unit so defined, raters will employ the sort of criteria they were intended to employ. Just because you and I agree in our identifications of instances of head-nods does not guarantee that in making decisions about each possible case we apply exactly the same criteria. (You might be considering only physical movement while I might be considering whether the interactant is intending to convey assent or not. No test of 'observables' could resolve the question.)

In fact, this would appear to lead to the conclusion that it is better to use categories which are *not* part of the rater's culture than those that are. For, in ordinarily applying terms such as 'smile', 'gesture', and 'question' to the description of behaviour it is natural in our culture to consult such 'unob-servables' as presumed intention, state of mind, meaning, etc. We should not expect even the most highly trained raters to ignore those cultural habits when, in the laboratory setting, they are asked to identify instances of the categories named. In this respect, an ostensive definition of 'alpha' might stand a better chance of escaping from an understanding in terms of 'unobservables' then those terms which are part of the rater's culture.

This raises a further question. One reason why Duncan and Fiske urge that unobservables not be included in raters' recognition rules is that they 'take for granted an understanding of the very phenomena that are under investigation' (Duncan and Fiske, 1977, p. 17). But how is this any different for so-called observables such as 'smiling' or 'gesticulating'? Do the raters not need already to understand that a speaker's facial movement is a smile (rather than, say, a grimace) in order to be able to identify it as a smile? We know what smiles are, why people smile, and within given contexts, what they may be taken to mean. Does not Duncan and Fiske's insistence that the categories identified be part of the rater's culture amount to the same thing as demanding that they 'understand the phenomena being investigated'?

David Clarke is well aware of the complexities and importance of devising an adequate categorization of conversational events.

> This is the point at which most attempts at a sequence analysis run into difficulties. The final statement that the observed form of events has a certain pattern can only really mean that a number of quite distinct behavior sequences have been classified as being similar by the investigator. If the classification is ill founded then the whole analysis is void (Clarke, 1977, p. 48).

For this very reason, it is surprising that the categorization scheme which he finally adopts is chosen *a priori* instead of developed through observation. But, as we have already seen, this choice was forced upon him by the failure of his inductively-based experiments designed to reveal the speech act units of conversational organization.

One source of the obstacles preventing Clarke from working out classes of conversational units was his choice of speech acts as the relevant units. From Duncan and Fiske's perspective a speech act, such as a 'threat' or a 'promise', counts as an unobservable. Consequently, how can one expect there to be agreement between subjects as to which speech acts are similar and which different? In other words, Clarke's very choice of elemental unit prevented him from keeping to the inductive, observation-based methodology urged by Duncan and Fiske.

Instead the *a priori* categories adopted by Clarke derive their existence from the terms English uses as performative verbs: e.g. 'promise', 'threat', 'insult', 'apologize', etc. There is, of course, no guarantee that for every such term there exists a conversational unit as its unique referent, or indeed that two subjects will both understand a particular term to refer to the same such units. Nevertheless, Clarke appears not to regard this as a drawback. Instead, he argues that it is an advantage of this approach that the terms used do not have to be given precise definitions or even ostensive definitions.

In a way this allows us to by-pass the details of the constitution of categories for the time being, because the names do not have to specify exactly what is to count as a *threat* or a *promise*. If sufficiently ambiguous definitions are given for the category names, then it is up to the subjects to identify each category when it occurs, or to see how a given abstract category could be represented in a particular form of words, making reference to context if need be (Clarke, 1983, p. 157).

It thus appears that, having failed with an inductive approach in working out categories of conversational units, Clarke decides to adopt the categorization provided by the names of performative verbs in English and that, in so doing, he avoids the problem of having to provide explicit definitions of recognitional criteria for the identification of each unit in particular conversations. Consequently, Clarke does not have to deal with the problem that inevitably would have arisen if he had succeeded in working out speech act categories by means of inductive methods: viz. Duncan and Fiske's problem of specifying criteria for identifying instances of the categories. Instead, his choice of names of performative verbs provides him automatically with a pre-established, culturally ratified set of implicit recognition rules. That is, he can rely on his subjects' cultural familiarity with the performative terms, and presumably with the categories of actions they are used to name, as sufficient to ensure their reliable identification of instances of those categories. Furthermore, this provides him with an 'emic' based approach which he prefers.

Of course, it is true that the implicit recognition rules on which Clarke relies themselves involve reference to what Duncan and Fiske would call unobservables. Nevertheless, Clarke uses a similar argument to that used by Duncan and Fiske: the proof that implicit recognition rules (even those involving unobservables) are adequate for the purpose of identifying instances of particular conversational units lies in the general agreement between raters in their identification of the relevant units.

Here we shall be investigating speech-act sequences in the assumption that clear regularities will only appear if subjects are consistent in their recognition of the speech-act types themselves (Clarke, 1983, p. 157).

In other words, if subjects acting as raters are consistent in identifying instances of 'threats', 'promises', 'insults', and the like (or, for that matter, 'smiles', 'head-nods', 'gesticulating', etc.) then it may be inferred

(a) that the subjects all understand the relevant terms ('threat', 'smile', etc.) in the same way;
(b) that they all implicitly understand the same categorization of conversational units;

(c) that their mutual understanding and use of both the terms and the categories they denote is proof that the system of terms used is an accurate reflection of the system of behavioural units described.

There is a fundamental mistake in this reasoning. It may best be illustrated by an analogy. Those familiar with the game of chess may well agree on the system of rules defining the possible moves of the various pieces; but no one takes this agreement as an indication that the system of possible moves is somehow an accurate reflection of a further system of rules, the units of which the chess pieces denote (e.g. the system of social positions in the medieval state). So why should the subjects' agreement on the use of the terms 'threat', 'insult', and so on be taken to indicate that that system of rules-of-use reflects some other system (i.e. conversational structure), the units of which are denoted by the terms concerned?

Nevertheless, a similar assumption is made in modern linguistics where subjects' agreement over the application of the terms 'grammatical' and 'ungrammatical' is taken as confirmation of an inherent difference between the possible sentences to which those terms are applied. And yet it turns out that subjects will often regularly use sentences that, when asked, they would label as 'ungrammatical', at the same time insisting that they would never use such sentences. Now, this leaves the theorist with two options. Either we may say that the subjects are incorrectly reporting the facts of the matter, or that grammaticality is not a property of sentences but rather of a learned system for talking about sentences. In either case, the upshot is that the agreed system for distinguishing sentences into two groups—the 'grammatical' and the 'ungrammatical'—may not be taken as derived from or as a reflection of the system of inherent distinctions between the sentences themselves. (To see this point, one only need consider that, if asked, ordinary speakers would probably identify the vowel in 'put' and that in 'nut' as instances of the same vowel. However, no linguist could accept this classification as a reflection of the inherent classes of the phonology of English.)

The same argument should be applied to the use of Duncan and Fiske's implicit recognition rules or of Clarke's names of performative verbs. It must not be presumed in advance that the conventions governing metalinguistic descriptions of conversational behaviour are determined by and reflect the 'actual facts' (whatever they may be) of conversational structure. In spite of what these metalinguistic conventions would lead us to assume, is it not possible that conversational behaviour is *not* inherently divisible into discrete 'chunks' or that what conversationalists (following those metalinguistic conventions) will uniformly describe as instances of the same event are *not* in fact so? If, as the social psychologists do, we want to study the true 'facts of the matter' of conversational behaviour, we should not derail our investigation from the start by assuming that, in our ordinary descriptive terms referring to that behaviour, we possess an accurate representation of those facts.

This is not to deny the importance of metalinguistic descriptions, nor their essential place in the study of conversation. We are simply arguing that their important role not be misinterpreted via the implicit acceptance of a surrogational theory of names: i.e. the theory that words have meaning because they 'stand-in' for the things they name. Only when it is cut loose from this assumption may the study of metalinguistics be appropriately pursued.

Where does this leave the task of identification in the social psychological study of conversation? Explicit recognition rules, as we have seen, may well be reliable 'identifiers', but it is far from clear what they identify, or indeed whether what they do may be properly called 'identification'. That is to say, in the study of conversational behaviour the more explicit ('objective', 'etic') an identification process becomes, the less useful it becomes because no longer does it accomplish anything we would ordinarily recognize as identification. There is a further, although related, problem with 'etic-based' explicit recognition rules: viz. that it is not obvious whether a 'non-emic' criterion can pick out anything of interest in conversational interaction where such a criterion would be unavailable to the participants themselves and thus not a part of their own identifying methods.

Implicit criteria, on the other hand, do not reliably tell researchers anything about the actual phenomena they believe themselves to be studying. This is true regardless of whether the criteria used involve reference to unobservables. Thus it would appear that inductively-based identification procedures are caught on the horns of a dilemma: either they identify reliably, but we may not be sure what it is they so identify; or they fail to identify at all and only reflect the metalinguistic conventions regulating the descriptive labels used.

The second distinctive feature pertaining to the inductive approach used in the social psychological study of conversation is the attempt to discover, by inductive, empirical analysis, the rules regulating conversational interaction. The reasoning behind this approach is disarmingly simple. It is assumed that the rules governing conversation will introduce patterned regularities into those areas of conversational behaviour which they govern. These regularities may be observed and measured according to statistical procedures. From any statistically significant regularity the investigator may hypothesize a version of the rule which is assumed to have produced that regularity. In further experiments, the hypothetical rule may be tested to see if it provides a satisfactory explanation of the behaviour it is proposed to govern.

The underlying conception of the research was that a given organization in face-to-face interaction would introduce marked regularities into the actions subject to that organization. If such were the case, then why not evaluate the proposed regularities by appropriate statistical tests? (Duncan and Fiske, 1977, p. 142).

This is the approach adopted by Duncan and Fiske and, in the stochastic study, by Clarke. The approach of Clarke's test-frame study is quite different because it focuses on the *possibility* of certain sequential relations holding between units (i.e. may X possibly be inserted in the context a —— b?) rather than on the statistical probability of those relationships. In most cases, rules hypothesized on the basis of possible sequences, such as the phrase structure rules postulated in the later stages of distributionalist syntax, will be quite different from those founded on the significant probability of sequences occurring. And, for the test-frame type of study, with its interest in sequential possibilities, the crucial question is whether it is legitimate and feasible to distinguish between possible ('well-formed') sequences and impossible ('non-well-formed') sequences. If it were not, then phrase structure grammars, such as those written in distributional and generative syntactic studies, could not be written. On the other hand, the crucial question for probability-based studies, such as the 'structural' and 'stochastic' studies, is not one of well-formedness, but rather is the question of inferring the existence of governing rules from the identification of statistical regularities. Since this latter question is particularly characteristic of the inductive methodology of social psychology, it is the one we will consider here.

Suppose a particular sequence of behaviour events is observed: X followed by Y. Ninety percent of the time which an X occurs, it is followed by a Y. (Obviously, we assume here no difficulty in identifying instances of Xs and Ys.) In such circumstances, the researcher following the inductive approach of the 'structural' and 'stochastic' studies would be led to hypothesize that the sequence XY is governed by the rule: if an X occurs, follow it by a Y. Our question is this: given the existence of such a statistical regularity, is it justified to hypothesize the existence of an underlying rule governing that regularity?

The crucial point to be made here is that it does not seem plausible to say that all regularities (even the most probable) are rule-governed; consequently, it becomes an issue to determine which are so governed and which are not. For example, suppose that, when I tie my shoes in the morning, it just so happens that over 90% of the time I tie my left one before I tie my right one. This could certainly be called a habit; but am I following a rule? A more complex example might be imagined. In the control room of the Central Electricity Generating Board, at any hour of the day or night, we might imagine that someone has the job of ensuring (among other things) that Oxford is allocated the required amount of electricity appropriate for the time of day or night. Over the years, we may imagine, the C.E.G.B. have developed detailed knowledge of Oxford's changing electrical requirements. They know, for example, that on a winter's morning, when the thermometer registers $-4°$ centigrade at 6 a.m. that between n and n^1 number of watts will regularly be needed for the hours between 7 a.m. to 9 a.m. In addition, they know that these figures only hold for weekday mornings because on weekends the needs are less and the hours are later. Indeed, we may imagine that the C.E.G.B. have a complex, sensitive theory of Oxford's electrical needs as they vary with time, weather, season, population patterns, work habits, and many other variables. We may in fact suppose that, because they use a computer in order to help them determine the amount of energy needed at any particular time, the C.E.G.B. have developed a complex system of rules (encoded in the language used by the computer) for predicting what we might call the electricity-oriented behaviour of the people of Oxford. Would it not, however, be entirely misguided to hypothesize that these rules, no matter how accurate they are, actually govern the electricity-oriented behaviour of any one citizen of Oxford? How indeed could the President of Trinity's act of switching on his desk lamp be governed by a rule formulated in the board-room of the C.E.G.B.? And if the C.E.G.B.'s rule does not govern the behaviour of any individual citizen of Oxford, how could the population as a whole be so governed? We must therefore draw the conclusion that some regularities of human behaviour, even extremely complex and highly predictable regularities, are not governed by rules.

Given then that, for example, the analysis performed by Duncan and Fiske of subjects' behaviour before and after the exchange of conversational turns led to the identification of many regularities, what is distinctive about these regularities that should permit us to say of them, but not of those observed in electricity use in Oxford, that they are rule-governed?

The point of this argument is that, if neither Duncan nor Fiske nor Clarke offer further evidence that the regularities they have discovered *are* rule-governed, then their hypotheses of an underlying system of conversational rules must be taken as unsupported, i.e. simply as guesses which are not required for the explanation of the regularities concerned. At the same time, they must remain unfalsifiable hypotheses, assuming that the regularities are consistent. There is no way to falsify the hypothesis that the regular behaviour of Oxford electricity users is governed by rules, for the very reason that no criterion can be found by which to distinguish between rule-governed and non-rule-governed regularities. If no criterion distinguishes rule-governed from 'free' regularities, then there is no way of falsifying the claim that some observed regularities are rule-governed. However, if examples may be found, such as the C.E.G.B. example where the postulation of a system of governing rules seems *prima facie* implausible, then the onus must be on those who wish to hypothesize underlying systems of rules for other regularities to justify the grounds for that hypothesis. No such justification is offered either by Clarke or by Duncan and Fiske.

Consequently, the inductive methods of sequential analysis, exemplified by the work of Duncan and Fiske and of Clarke, should fairly be seen only to have observed certain patterns of regularities, perhaps even to have 'discovered' regularities which are in fact characteristic of at least some sequences of conversational units. But to say that these regularities are the product of an underlying organization, or system of rules, governing conversational behaviour, is to depart from the inductivist, experimental methodology characteristic of the social psychological tradition and to leap into the realm of the speculative. By abandoning the inductive approach just at this point, and declaring the stochastic study to be disappointing, Clarke tacitly admits that he has reached the limits of the domain of inductive methodology and that the sought-after units and rules of conversational organization lie outside the purview of that domain.

As the next three chapters deal with models of conversation analysis which have also rejected the inductive method in favour of the hypothetico-deductive, we will reserve our comments on the latter method until we have discussed its exemplars in full. We begin with an approach which has already been mentioned in connection with the work of David Clarke: conversation analysis using speech act theory.

3

Speech Act Theory and Conversation Analysis

In Chapter 2 we encountered the idea, central to the whole rules and units approach, that conversation can best be analysed as a series of discrete acts, sequentially organized. Like the social psychologists we were considering, we concentrated on the problems associated with identifying and categorizing these conversational acts. We examined, for instance, the arguments surrounding the use of emic versus etic criteria, and whether etic criteria can be totally 'observable'; we also discussed the methodological issue of whether induction is useful, or even feasible, in analysing conversational data. Many of the ideas which are central to this book have thus been introduced already; in this third chapter we shall have occasion to return to the same basic questions again. Our main preoccupation will be with matters of taxonomy and identification of acts in conversation, but we shall be concerned with a particular perspective on such acts, a perspective deriving from philosophical writing on *speech acts*. The conversation analysts we consider in this chapter resemble each other in adopting the idea that the basic elements of conversation, the acts or events from which it is built up, should be analysed as *illocutionary acts* as defined in the work of J. L. Austin and John Searle. This is also, of course, the very conclusion arrived at by the social psychologist David Clarke; and since we have already discussed his work in some detail, we may usefully take it as a point of departure in several of the sections which make up this chapter. However, the models to be considered here in detail are those of Edmondson (1981) and Labov and Fanshel (1977), together with the theoretical writings of Searle. These writers have had to pay a great deal of attention to the problems rather cavalierly brushed aside by Clarke.

One task which we do not intend to undertake is the minute exposition of speech act theory and the exhaustive surveying of its voluminous literature. The work of Searle and Austin has been taken up for many different purposes within linguistics, most notably by general semantics and pragmatics (for a summary from the viewpoint of pragmatic theory, see Levinson, 1983, chapter 5). We hope this has made its most important concepts sufficiently familiar to readers of this book: we propose to confine ourselves to the use of speech act theory in structural conversation analysis, and indeed to reserve our detailed commentary for those aspects of the theory which illustrate our thesis about rules and units, and the problems they raise. As far as we know this is a novel approach, the rules and units tendencies in speech act theory having received very little overt attention.

Speech acts: a rules and units approach?

As is well known, the foundations of speech act theory were laid by the philosopher J. L. Austin in his 1955 series of William James lectures, *How To Do Things With Words* (Austin, 1962; 2nd ed. 1975). These foundations have been built on by John Searle in particular: since Searle has fleshed out many of Austin's suggestions, it is his work which has received most attention from conversation analysts, and which will be our main focus here.

The central assertion made by speech act theorists is that to speak is not only to *say* something but to *do* something. Austin distinguishes between the locutionary act, that is the act of producing a form of words with sense, reference and so on, and the *illocutionary* act of investing utterances with some communicative force (e.g. as promises, warnings, assertions or requests). He also refers to *perlocutionary* acts achieved by speaking: for instance, an assertion may have the perlocutionary effect of persuading the hearer that something is the case, or a warning may prevent the hearer from doing something. These three types of act must be distinguished from each other, and all may admit of a detailed analysis. The analyst of language, in particular, must concern herself with the conventions for illocution as well as locution. Searle (1969, p. 17) underlines this point with an analogy:

> A theory of language is part of a theory of action, simply because speaking is a rule-governed form of behaviour. Now, being rule-governed, it has formal features that admit of independent study. But a study purely of those formal features, without a study of their role in speech acts, would be like study of the currency and credit systems of economics without a study of the role of currency and credit in economic transactions.

Just as one describes the moves of a game, or the behaviour of people in the economic sphere, with an awareness that acts are purposeful and goal-directed, so it has to be acknowledged that in verbal interaction, utterances further the interests of actors. Searle suggests that utterances can do this because they are recognizable tokens of illocutionary act-types. Illocutions themselves 'come off' because speakers can recognize them, via shared knowledge of the types and their conditions of production. Or put another way, of units and rules.

The significance of this for the analysis of conversation is immediately obvious. If it is indeed the case that utterances form part of the purposeful and rational exchanges of everyday life by virtue of the fact that they perform illocutionary acts, perhaps natural conversation can be viewed as a sequence of such acts. The illocutionary act, in other words, may be the primitive unit of conversation. A description which takes this idea as its starting point is then committed to the following three questions: first, what speech acts exist in a language, second, what are the rules for producing and interpreting them, and third, what are the rules for sequencing them coherently? These questions remind us of the problems we have already come up against in relation to other models: deciding on suitable classes of act, determining which utterances instantiate which acts, and investigating whether language-users 'know' the rules, or follow them.

In the remainder of this chapter we will pursue these problems in two main sections. First, we will look at the classification and recognition of illocutionary acts, which has been a major headache for philosophers and conversation analysts alike. Secondly, we will turn our attention to the problem of sequence, which is less of a thorn in the sides of philosophers, but is crucial to empirical analyses of talk.

Classification and recognition of illocutionary acts

The reader will recall that in his later work David Clarke abandoned the quest for a classified set of conversational acts arrived at by induction, and decided instead to make use of a set which he defined *a priori* and labelled with familiar metalinguistic terms for illocutionary acts (e.g. *requests*). It will also be remembered that Clarke made the rather odd assumption that this

> . . . allows us to bypass the details of the constitution of categories for the time being, because the names do not have to specify exactly what counts as a *threat* or a *promise*.

And he goes on,

> If sufficiently ambiguous definitions are given for the category names, then it is up to the subjects to identify each category as it occurs, or to see how a given abstract category could be represented in a particular form of words, making reference to context if need be (Clarke, 1983, p. 157).

We have already pointed out some of the things that are wrong with this. It depends on there being an unproblematic correspondence between the facts of conversational structure and the names people use to describe it. Furthermore, it is only analytically useful if it turns out people agree on the use of speech-act names, and *if that agreement is taken as evidence for the existence of shared, unobservable criteria for the use of the names/identification of the categories they refer to*. If such agreement were not forthcoming, or if it were just an accidental regularity not produced by any shared criteria, the taxonomy of categories posited by Clarke would not be generalizable to all instances of conversation; indeed, the whole project of constructing taxonomies would be rendered quite pointless in a case of this sort. It is therefore not at all surprising to discover that almost all analysts using the notion 'illocutionary act' or 'speech act' assume that there is some shared core of meaning to the acts which are designated by a specific name, and that there are shared criteria for identifying those acts.

Searle's approach to classification

Searle's whole approach to the illocutionary act is dependent on the way he conceptualizes communication in general. The speech act is essentially a conventional channel by which communication is achieved:

> In the case of speech acts performed within a language . . . it is a matter of convention—as opposed to strategy, technique, procedure, or natural fact—that the utterance of such and such expressions under certain conditions counts as the making of a promise (Searle, 1969, p. 37).

The task of the analyst is first and foremost to locate the acts which may be performed in speech, and to state the conditions ('felicity conditions') under which the utterance of particular expressions will be taken, conventionally, as instantiating certain acts.

An example may be helpful here. In his book *Speech Acts* (1969), Searle analyses the felicity conditions for performing the speech act of *promising*. He notes that the utterance *I promise that p* is a conventional realisation of the act of promising: but it can only *be* that act under certain conditions. For example, the speaker must sincerely commit herself to an undertaking to perform some act at some future time. The act must be something the hearer would like the speaker to do, and something it is not obvious the speaker will do anyway. If conditions such as these (see Searle, 1969, pp. 57–61, for a full account of how to promise) are not met, then the utterance will not be taken as a promise. For instance, if I promise you something you clearly do not want, as I well know—if I utter, for instance, *I promise to beat you to a pulp if you laugh at my shoes again*, my 'promise' may be taken as a warning or threat (this underlines our earlier point, that metalinguistic expressions do not simply and monotonically denote single acts on every occasion of use). If

I say *I promise I'll come to work fully clothed tomorrow*, I may be interpreted as having made a joke. The reason why my utterance communicates my intention to promise (or threaten, or joke) is precisely that we share the conventions for producing and recognizing these acts.

This question of intention is very important, for intentions are at bottom what conventional acts exist to convey. For Searle, in fact, it defines communication that the hearer must recognize the speaker's intention. This condition is both necessary and sufficient for the successful performance of illocutionary acts, as the following remark demonstrates (Searle, 1969, p. 47):

> If I am trying to tell someone something, then . . . as soon as he recognises that I am trying to tell him something and exactly what it is I am trying to tell him, I have succeeded in telling it to him. . . . In the case of illocutionary acts we succeed in doing what we are trying to do by getting our audience to recognise what we are trying to do. But the 'effect' on the hearer is not a belief or response, it consists simply in the hearer understanding the utterance of the speaker.

Illocutionary force is a matter of the intentions of the speaker, which must then be accurately recovered by the hearer. This axiom has led to the obvious objection that speakers' intentions are not always clear, and that since they are private we have no way of knowing if we have interpreted them correctly. Strawson comments (1971, p. 24):

> Given that we know the meaning of an utterance, there may still be a further question as to how what was said was meant by the speaker, or as to how the words spoken were used, or as to how the utterance was to be taken or ought to be taken. In order to know the illocutionary force of the utterance, we must know the answer to this further question.

It is precisely this *impasse* that a rules and units approach is meant to resolve: granted that the hearer is not telepathic, the analyst may simply have recourse to that familiar device, the shared set of rules. In other words, when speaker X makes a promise, Y takes it to be a promise because s/he has some way of looking up X's utterance in a mental typology of illocutionary acts which is identical in all respects to X's typology. Having assigned the utterance to the class of promises, Y is also able to decide whether the promise itself is a valid one, because s/he shares the rules according to which X made it.

Searle assumes that to communicate successfully, speakers must get each other to 'recognize what we are trying to do', that is to say, what illocutionary act is being performed/what illocutionary force some utterance possesses. He further suggests that this recognition is possible because conversationalists share the constitutive rules for a set of acts, and knowledge of the linguistic conventions whereby each act can be realized in practice. For such assumptions and suggestions to have any utility in actually analysing conversation, it seems we need a proposal as to what the set of illocutionary acts performable in talk is, together with some evidence that conversationalists really do recognize just these acts, and a statement of the criteria which permit them to do so. In other words, we must embark on a primarily definitional and typological project.

Philosophers of language have not been slow to realize the magnitude and difficulty of the task of constructing illocutionary typologies. Austin calculated (1975, p. 150) that if we began by simply picking out the illocutionary verbs from a standard English dictionary, we would end up with a list of between one thousand and ten thousand speech acts. He himself approached the problem by proposing (rather hesitantly and provisionally, it seems) a small number of speech act 'families' (see Austin, 1975, p. 151ff). A similar approach is also adopted by Searle in his 1975 article on classifying illocutionary acts.

In this article, Searle divides illocutions into major classes based mainly on their 'essential condition'. For instance, stating and complaining belong to the category of *assertives*, which can generally be subsumed under the proposition 'S is committed to the truth of p.' Commanding and requesting, in contrast, are *directives*, in which the speaker intends that the hearer produce some effect; promising and offering are *commissives* ('S is committed to a future act A'), while thanking, forgiving, blaming and so on are *expressives* in which S makes known her/his attitude to the hearer. Searle assumes these essential conditions for the performance of various illocutionary acts are conventions all members of a community share; indeed he has occasionally made the much stronger claim that, when pared down to essentials in this way, speech acts are universal:

> Different human languages, to the extent they are intertranslatable, can be regarded as different conventional realizations of the same underlying rules (Searle, 1969, p. 39).

This kind of approach, which is clearly etic or analyst oriented as opposed to emic or participant oriented, begs two questions, one of them prior to the other. Firstly, it may be asked whether participants do actually share a repertoire of speech acts to the extent Searle is claiming, or indeed their underlying constitutive rules. This is tantamount to asking whether the etic approach is valid at all, since it proposes that we judge Searle's taxonomic categories by their degree of correspondence to the categories recognized by conversationalists themselves. Secondly, if we agree to accept a particular set of categories, we need to spell out in more detail than Searle does how conversationalists in actual speech situations identify utterances as instances of acts.

Since in fact very few conversation analysts have questioned the validity of the whole procedure of constructing illocutionary taxonomies, we will begin by considering the second question in relation to two empirical studies using classifications of illocutionary acts. These studies are Labov and Fanshel's *Therapeutic Discourse* (1977) and Edmondson's *Spoken Discourse, A Model for Analysis* (1981). After examining their approach to the question of how conversationalists get, in Labov and Fanshel's phrase, 'from utterance to act', we will return to the first question of whether conversationalists share a set of speech acts and criteria for recognizing them, looking in particular at the critique of Searle produced by Marga Kreckel (1981).

Labov and Fanshel

Therapeutic Discourse is an extended attempt to analyse a piece of interactional data: it deals with a single, fifteen-minute extract from a therapist's regular interview with her client. Labov and Fanshel point out the affinities between their approach to conversation analysis and the speech act framework of Austin and Searle. They view interaction as a non-random sequence of speech acts, and are thus very closely concerned with the classification and identification of speech act types.

Labov and Fanshel are unusually cautious in assessing the limits of conversation analysis. They do not believe that speech act types form a closed set, nor that anyone could construct a well-defined set of mappings between speech acts and syntactic units (sentences or utterances). This means that a 'grammar of conversation' is not a useful or even attainable objective:

> Our aim is to produce a reasonable accounting, after the fact, which will embody as many general principles as we can find (Labov and Fanshel, 1977, p. 358).

This does not mean, however, that Labov and Fanshel are not in the business of discovering rules and units. On the contrary, it is the location of various acts, and the formulation of rules or 'general principles' for identifying examples of them, which constitute 'reasonable accounting' in their view. Like the other analysts we have considered, they take it for granted that participants in talk (in this case, in the speech event 'therapeutic interview') possess the means (shared conventions or principles) to understand each other's utterances in similar ways: to recognize, say, the act of 'challenging' by activating a network of shared rules and assumptions about the existence, production and interpretation of challenges. It is implicitly claimed throughout Labov and Fanshel's book that one problem with clients in therapeutic interviews is their tendency to misrecognize, either inadvertently or strategically, the conventional import of others' remarks, while veiling the force of their own behind equally devious clouds of indirection. One aim of the therapy is to clear up these problems: thus the therapist or analyst in some sense becomes the arbiter of what is 'really going on' in talk.

How then do Labov and Fanshel elucidate 'what is really going on' in a piece of talk? First of all, they take it that a number of things are going on at once. The reason why there cannot be one-to-one mappings between utterances and speech acts is that

> most utterances can be seen as performing several speech acts at once (1977, p. 29).

They therefore analyse utterances as sets of hierarchically structured acts, from the most abstract to the most superficial. Take, for instance, an utterance produced by the client in Labov and Fanshel's data, Rhoda: Rhoda reports having said to her mother

Well, when d'you plan to come home?

Superficially, this might be analysed as a request for information. More abstractly, or indirectly, it is a request for action: Rhoda is asking her mother to come home. At a deeper level still, however, and the one Labov and Fanshel are most interested in, the utterance is a *challenge*. Rhoda hints that her mother *should* come home because as a mother and head of the household, her primary responsibility is to be there. To analyse the remark as a challenge, we judge it not only in relation to background knowledge of a local kind (these particular participants, their situations and histories) but also in relation to a broader understanding of social roles and obligations— an understanding the participants (allegedly) share.

Of course, the problem raised by this hierarchical analysis of speech acts is how conversationalists themselves know that a particular utterance should be treated as instantiating a specific, deep-level act. That is to say, how do participants in talk perform this kind of analysis for themselves (it is open to doubt, of course, *whether* they do; but Labov and Fanshel assume, as usual, that the organized nature of conversational interaction can only be explained by supposing that is what happens). Aware that they need to provide some mechanism whereby conversationalists recognize deep acts, Labov and Fanshel formulate what they call 'rules of discourse'.

Labov and Fanshel's 'rules of discourse' are an attempt to specify how conversationalists get from utterance to act. They provide

> a model of how speakers might go about producing and interpreting these hierarchical structures of speech actions (1977, p. 357).

They take the form: If A makes a remark to B and the following conditions hold ($C_1, C_2, \ldots, C_n$), hear the remark as an X (where X is some category of act). A concrete example is the rule whereby any statement by A about an event that is part of B's biography or acknowledged sphere of expertise will be heard by B as a request for confirmation.

This sort of rule brings up a new problem (which is also faced by the ethnomethodologists, and which we will therefore be returning to in Chapter 6 below). It is the problem of how one can possibly check that conversationalists are following the rule one has hypothesized. Obviously, few lay conversationalists are likely to come up with Labov and Fanshel's formula in response to a friendly enquiry from the analyst. But equally obviously from our point of view, mere regular behaviour in particular situations is insufficient to confirm the existence of a specific rule. It is always possible to formulate a number of rules according to which one's data make perfect sense; but it is very difficult to evaluate the alternatives in any sensible, let alone conclusive way.

Let us illustrate this point with an example from our own data which could be taken as exemplifying Labov and Fanshel's rule that statements about 'B events' are taken as requests for confirmation. In the following short extract, B is a priest and A lives in his house.

> A: You're lucky you don't have to go to work today.
> B: Well I've got to go to Evensong.

Certainly, this extract could be read as fitting the rule hypothesized by Labov and Fanshel. A makes a remark about a 'B-event', namely B's obligations regarding work that day. B hears it as a request for confirmation, but withholds confirmation because the remark is inaccurate. *Well* on this account might be taken as a polite hedge, or a marker of the fact that to disagree is a 'face threatening act' and therefore 'dispreferred' (see Chapter 6). But equally, it could be read in other ways, no less plausible than the initial hypothesis. Perhaps B heard A's remark as a challenge; perhaps he suspected A issued it with an ulterior motive (thus he might be trying to forestall a suggestion that since he does not have to work, he might mow the lawn or clean the house). In this case, B frames his reply in anticipation of possible future moves by A, and this involves acting as if he heard A's comment as a challenge.

But if this is what is happening, an unsuspected difficulty in analysing talk appears. Once an analyst is accountable to some specific body of data, decisions as to what a remark was 'heard as' must be taken at least partly on the basis of the hearer's response to it. Yet this is hardly an infallible guide to the *hearing* of the original remark. Whatever a hearer takes a remark to mean or imply, she may choose to treat it in any number of ways (the point of this being, for instance, to anticipate requests one does not wish to comply with, or to avoid conceding an opponent's point). Thus if a hearer does not respond to a remark in the way Labov and Fanshel's 'rules of discourse' imply she should, we cannot say the remark was definitely heard as an 'X'; but it is also impossible to be sure it was not.

In the end the analysts cannot produce good evidence, even from such detailed data as theirs, that a remark has in fact been heard as any particular category of act. Without such evidence it is difficult to see what makes one rule-hypothesis superior to another. It is also impossible to give much support to the familiar central assumption that co-conversationalists actually do interpret utterances and acts in similar ways; which raises the question once again whether shared rules, conventions or principles are needed to explain the communicative behaviour and experience of participants in talk.

Edmondson

The second model we must consider here is that of Willis Edmondson (1981). In *Spoken Discourse: A Model for Analysis*, Edmondson attempts to devise a comprehensive description of a fairly large corpus of 'conversational' data (we use scare quotes here because Edmondson's corpus is actually somewhat bizarre: rather than naturally-occurring talk, it consists of a series of elicited dialogues. Student informants were given imaginary roles and situations (e.g. 'Sheila wishes to borrow records off a flatmate') within which to produce interaction (Edmondson, 1981, p. 77). To this methodology we would apply some of the strictures we applied earlier to the work of the social psychologists. There is no guarantee that data obtained in this way is representative of talk produced in non-experimental contexts).

Edmondson shares with Labov and Fanshel his selection of the illocutionary act as a fundamental conversational unit. In other ways, however, he diverges in his approach from the method adopted in *Therapeutic Discourse*. He believes, for instance, that analysis is impossible unless we take it as axiomatic that each utterance has only one illocutionary force, and he criticizes Labov and Fanshel for thinking otherwise. He is also a much more outspoken proponent of the view that illocutionary taxonomies should be etic, totally discounting all judgements made by participants as pretheoretical and unexplicated.

So important is this principle of etic analysis to Edmondson, he rejects the use of the standard illocutionary verbs as labels for types of act. We must beware of people's own characterizations of their behaviour, expressed in misleading and untrustworthy expressions like *promise*, *ask a question*, etc., and

> find appropriate technical terms to describe such acts rather than relying on the denotations of existing lexical items of English (1981, p. 30).

This stance of Edmondson's is slightly reminiscent of the condemnation of *unobservables* by Duncan and Fiske (see Chapter 1). It leaves Edmondson in a peculiarly difficult position when it comes to producing an illocutionary taxonomy and criteria for the analyst to classify acts by, since if the use of our normal metalinguistic intuitions is outlawed, Edmondson needs to provide more than usually explicit criteria for using 'appropriate technical terms'— which he must also go to the trouble of inventing. (As we shall see later in this chapter, his task is made even more difficult by the fact that he refuses to employ the most obvious etic cues—those relating to an utterance's position in discourse—in classifying illocutionary function.)

Nevertheless, Edmondson makes the attempt: in order to describe his corpus of spoken discourse, he defines 'objectively' eighteen separate acts, and labels them with appropriate names (disappointingly, these turn out to be 'existing lexical items of English', some of them suspiciously like the standard illocutionary verbs (e.g. *apologize*); but the reader is under strict instructions to go by the detailed definitions he provides, and not her ordinary use of these words). He then applies these exhaustively defined categories to the analysis of his data as a series of illocutions.

However, if empirical adequacy in describing the data is to be the measure of Edmondson's success, it must be said at once that the analyses he makes are open to very strong objection. There are two main grounds on which we might object: first, it is unclear where the eighteen acts 'come from' and whether they have any relevance for Edmondson's subjects; while second, the analysis itself is not reliably replicable using Edmondson's own definitions of particular acts. Reading Edmondson's descriptions, it is often quite obscure why specific utterances have been classified as they have.

The first objection is bound to come up in relation to any etic classification; and as we have seen, that is the only kind Edmondson finds acceptable. The question is, how can an analyst decide that this set of categories and no other is the best description of his data? In this case, it appears the categories have simply been induced from the data, but on what basis remains unstated. Clearly, criteria of exhaustiveness and parsimony may be invoked (i.e. the analyst looks for the fewest categories which nevertheless account for all the data), but the selection he makes, and the label he affixes to each category, is always open to the charge of arbitrariness, and of being unrevealing insofar as it has no relevance to the behaviour and the classifications of conversationalists themselves.

To demonstrate our second objection, let us examine part of one elicited dialogue as analysed by Edmondson. The situation given to the participants is as follows (p. 175):

> X returns to the seating position in a university library where she has been working to discover that her place has been occupied during her short absence by Y, that her books and working materials have been

moved to one side, and that there is no available alternative place (Edmondson, 1981, p. 175).

The extract given for this situation is reproduced below, leaving out all irrelevant parts of the analysis (i.e. everything but the actual utterances and the illocutionary label appended by Edmondson; if prosodic phenomena played any part at all in the illocutionary categorization this is not clear, and they are therefore omitted).

1	X:	well er I'm terribly sorry but er	APOLOGIZE
2		I'm afraid you're in my seat	COMPLAIN
3		you've moved my books	COMPLAIN
4	Y:	oh dear	EXCLAIM
3	X:	and papers	COMPLAIN
5		you must have realized somebody was here	COMPLAIN
6	Y:	oh that's er	EXCLAIM
7		well I looked around	EXCUSE
8		there wasn't anybody else any other space and er	EXCUSE
9	X:	Well I'm awfully sorry	APOLOGIZE
10	Y:	I waited a little while and nobody came	EXCUSE
11		I'm sorry if I've taken your place	APOLOGIZE

(Edmondson, 1981, p. 176)

There are a number of cases here in which Edmondson's assignment of an utterance to a certain category is impossible to reconcile with his own criteria for that category. For example, utterance 5 is rather oddly interpreted as a COMPLAIN, the condition for which is:

S wishes H to believe that S is not in favour of H's having performed some act A, as against the interests of S.

This category could well apply to utterances 2 and 3, but hardly to 5 where no act of H's is directly referred to. 5 fits better with the alternative category OPINE (pp. 145-6). It is also odd to assign 7, 8 and 10 to the category EXCUSE when this is defined:

S wishes H to believe that S is not fully accountable for the fact that he performed past action A, nor is he responsible for any consequences following that A.

For it is clear that S *is* accountable here: she has been caught in *flagrante delicto*, and what she is doing, though it would count as making an excuse in ordinary non-technical English, is giving reasons why her actions were justified, rather than denying responsibility for them. Edmondson seems to have been misled by the usual meaning of *excuse* into ignoring his own technical definition of it. Utterances 7, 8 and 10 are better classified as instances of JUSTIFY,

> S wishes H to know that S does not find action A for which he is responsible, socially discreditable.

Even this is not a totally satisfactory account of what is going on, however, since Y shows signs of knowing her behaviour *is* socially discreditable, even as she tries to justify it.

Finally, some comment must be made on the assignment of 9 (*well I'm awfully sorry*) to the category APOLOGIZE, which makes it equivalent to 11 (*I'm sorry if I've taken your place*). It is possible to argue they are not even similar in function: whereas 11 is a genuine or at least a functional apology, 9 seems to be merely a polite preface to a request that Y leave. A competent hearer might be expected to recognize the differing functions of 9 and 11.

The point of this assertion is not (or not only) that Edmondson has got his analysis wrong. Rather, it is of interest to ask what in principle he is to do when this situation arises. Clearly, as he defines APOLOGIZE, both 9 and 11 are members of that class. Edmondson's definition does allow that instances of APOLOGIZE can be used as disarmers: but who decides just which instances are being used in that way? In the end, the analyst's intuitions are crucial, and unless the classifications proliferate uncontrollably there will be problems capturing fine distinctions without resorting to the kind of 'unexplicated, pretheoretical' metalinguistic judgements Edmondson is so eager to avoid.

Edmondson aims at the principled assignment of an objective and unique illocutionary value to each move in talk; as the above comments suggest, the attempt is unsuccessful, but more fundamentally it is open to question whether the project is feasible at all.

It is also open to question whether it is necessary, and this brings us back to an issue we deferred earlier in this chapter. The sets of categories and the recognition rules we have been examining are necessitated by a certain theoretical orientation, one that takes it as axiomatic that there is intersubjective agreement on what speech acts are possible, what they mean and so on. As we have pointed out already, it is possible to maintain a sceptical position on this. One researcher who began her work from just such a position is the social psychologist Marga Kreckel.

The critique of Searle: Marga Kreckel

It will be remembered that the philosopher John Searle in 1975 put forward a taxonomy of illocutionary acts, defined by crucial parts of their felicity conditions. It will also be remembered that Searle made a claim for speech act types as linguistic universals:

Different human languages, to the extent they are intertranslatable, can be regarded as different conventional realizations of the same underlying rules (Searle, 1969, p. 39).

Both Searle's taxonomy, and the universalistic outlook which must inform the construction of etic typologies in general, have recently come under attack from a researcher working in social psychology, whose approach combines theoretical and empirical critique.

Marga Kreckel, in her study *Communicative Acts and Shared Knowledge in Natural Discourse* (1981), criticizes Searle on a number of grounds. She denies that speakers of a language all share typologies of illocutionary acts, and she argues that they do not necessarily have similar ideas about the interpretation of acts to which they do append similar labels (that is, even if we all agree that something is 'a promise', it may not be the case that we all define *promise* in the same way). Kreckel believes that typologies must be verified empirically, and that they must be 'emic' or participant-oriented. Under these methodological conditions, she claims, it will soon become clear that the conventions for performing and interpreting speech acts vary dramatically.

These conclusions of Kreckel's are based on an empirical study using data from the BBC 'fly on the wall' documentary, *Family*. Kreckel augmented the data from the programme with quasi-experimental work involving the family in question and also, for comparative purposes, another rather different family. Her main hypothesis is summed up in this statement (1981, p. 4):

> The degree of understanding potentially achieved in verbal exchanges is a direct function of the degree of convergence of the interactionally relevant concepts held by the interactors and their shared conventions for expressing them.

She suggests that ultimately, an individual arrives at a unique interpretation of any message; however, a set of individuals with a considerable body of shared knowledge, experience, norms and expectations (such as a family) will produce more consistent interpretations than a random group without this shared knowledge. To the extent that linguistic conventions are shared, they constitute what Kreckel calls a 'subcode'. Different subcodes may quite easily include differing definitions of speech acts and conventions for their performance.

To demonstrate that this is so, Kreckel asks the members of her two informant families to define the features of particular speech acts, then compares their definitions with each other, and with Searle's. The illocutionary type she chooses as an illustration is that of *warning*. She finds that in definitions of this act,

> there is complete overlap within one family, but a marked difference between families I and II (1981, p. 48).

Furthermore, both families differ from Searle, for whereas his definition of warning is 'an undertaking that some future event is not in the interest of the hearer', family I define it as getting the hearer to take evasive action, and family II place most emphasis on trying to influence the hearer for the speaker's own ends (Kreckel, 1981, pp. 48–60).

As Kreckel points out, this seriously challenges, Searle's taxonomy since both families regard 'warning' as a directive type, but Searle would not include it in that class. It seems then that Searle does not have 'the same underlying rules' for *warning* as families I and II, even leaving aside the question of whether he shares their conventions for performing warnings. He would not be able to identify the same utterances as warnings as Kreckel's subjects; and equally it appears he would interpret instances of warning, supposing these could be identified, rather differently from either of the families.

Kreckel is not arguing here that Searle's definition and criteria are wrong. Rather she is challenging the presumption of unlimited intersubjective agreement among speakers of a language upon which the entire quest for general criteria depends. As she says,

> Warnings in general do not exist. What counts as a 'warning' depends on rules evolved and sustained in concrete interaction within social groups (1981, p. 60).

This makes speech acts rather different from games (an analogy often drawn by Searle and others) since the rules of games are not evolved in this way. To attempt to construct a general taxonomy of illocutions is not, therefore, to extract some 'common core' from a few minor variants in the use of terms like *warning*. Rather, it is an illegitimate privileging of the analyst's own metalinguistic categories.

It seems to us that Kreckel's critique could be taken further and applied to her own work. For as the remark quoted above shows, Kreckel assumes a social-psychological universe of rule-governed behaviour in the manner of Harré ('what counts as a warning depends on rules . . . within social groups'). Yet it is not obvious that her informants are following rules, nor that we need to assume they are doing so in order to explain her empirical findings. Certainly, Kreckel's work demonstrates an impressive degree of intersubjective agreement about 'what counts as a warning' within each family (and equally impressive disagreement elsewhere). But this agreement need not be based on rules or conventions; since they arise, precisely, within a family, the regularities of behaviour reported by Kreckel could be produced by habit and experience, for example.

The work of Kreckel also raises questions about what our model of *communication* should be. Kreckel's findings indicate that the vast majority of interactions (those which do not take place between family members or other intimates) entail major differences of interpretation between the participants. Must we therefore say that communication does not actually occur in such interactions? Plainly, an assertion of that kind would be unfaithful to any common-sense view of what goes on in talk, and incompatible with the experience of participants. It would also be absurd inasmuch as it would force us to count almost all talk as being communicatively unsuccessful. But if this argument is sound, it means we must change our concept of what it means to communicate, rejecting in particular the assumption that communication is a matter of a one-to-one match between the speaker's intention and the hearer's interpretation.

Yet if that is accepted, it could be argued that there is no further motivation for rules and units anyway. Congruence between intention and interpretation is only explicable in terms of a shared system, mechanically employed by individual language-users; but if the theory rejects congruence on the grounds that there is none, it seems unnecessary to keep the apparatus whose function was to explain it.

By orienting his model to speakers' intentions, Searle commits himself to a theory of communication in which understanding is equivalent to recovering intention accurately. This necessitates a shared apparatus of units and rules. The models of conversation which take illocutionary acts as basic units are essentially concerned to discover, in relation to specific pieces of data, what the shared apparatus consists of. It is rarely asked whether the observed facts of speech demand such an apparatus at all. Thus in examining speech-act based descriptions of conversation it is important to ask what motivation exists for postulating shared rules and units as the basis of successful communication. It is necessary to bear in mind Kreckel's critique of Searle, too, examining the specific rules and units proposed in various models for signs that they merely project the analyst's own intuitions (the very ones that demand explanation) on to the data.

The problem of sequence in speech act-based conversation analysis

Although the notion that the illocutionary act is the basic unit of talk has been a productive one for empirical conversation analysts, especially those whose background is in structural linguistics, there is one respect in which the writings of philosophers have strikingly failed to provide much assistance. The question of how illocutionary acts are sequenced in actual episodes of connected speech is not one that looms large in the lives of philosophers, who tend to construct the examples they use, and to imagine each example in splendid isolation. For the analyst working with natural data, however, it is an issue on a par with that of classification/identification.

Indeed it is the 'next stage': as David Clarke notes, the analytic task falls into three parts, namely unitizing, categorizing and sequential analysis.

Clarke also illustrates the way in which many conversation analysts have used the model of grammatical structure to talk about doing sequential analysis, given the lack of any model in speech act theory proper. We have already quoted his remarks on this topic, but it is well worth considering them once again:

> The rules which generate all and only the speech act sequences which are sensible conversations are . . . like the rules which generate all and only the morpheme strings which are well-formed sentences (Clarke, 1983, p. 106).

Similar analogies with generative syntax are to be found in both the models we have considered already in this chapter. Labov and Fanshel claim, for instance, that

> the rules of discourse . . . are like the rules of syntax in their unconscious, invariant nature (1977, p. 75).

Edmondson formulates the objectives for an adequate description of conversation in the following, quasi-generative terms:

> It should be possible to formulate a set of discourse formulation rules which would recursively enumerate an unbounded number of interactional structures. Both system-networks and rewrite rule systems could generate such structures (Edmondson, 1981, p. 190).

These analysts also believe that sequence is the central problem for a linguistic analysis of conversation; in the words of Labov and Fanshel (1977, p. 69):

> The central problem of discourse analysis is to discover the connexions between utterances . . . [and later on (p. 299)] . . . how utterances follow each other in rational, rule-governed manner.

It is clear from these quotations (and many others could be found) that sequencing of units—in the case of the analysts we are concerned with, illocutionary acts—is believed to be governed by quasi-grammatical rules. It is therefore of interest to explore the question of how such a belief is made operational in the models of Labov and Fanshel and of Edmondson.

Labov and Fanshel, somewhat surprisingly, sidestep the whole question of surface sequence, and are vague on the issue of sequence in general. Their position is a consequence of their claim, already discussed, that every speech act should be given a hierarchical analysis: although sequencing of illocutionary acts is rule-governed, the rules do not apply to the superficial levels, but rather to the deepest underlying acts. So Rhoda's utterance *When d'you plan to come home*, which Labov and Fanshel analyse as (ultimately) a challenge, will be followed by an utterance realizing an act which may be analysed as the sort of act that naturally follows challenges: an 'admission', perhaps, or a 'defence'. Since all the deep act categories may be realized by any number of surface illocutions, which in turn may be realized by a profusion of syntactic structures, a sequence which is orderly at the deepest level may produce startling discontinuity or incoherence at the surface. So long as this is resolvable via a more penetrating analysis of 'what is really going on', i.e. what act is actually being performed, Labov and Fanshel are unworried by it. (This also, incidentally, makes the classification problem more acute. For if conversationalists are sequencing acts rather than utterances, thus producing surface discontinuity which does not result in conversational breakdown, they must have shared knowledge of just which utterances instantiate which acts.)

Not surprisingly, given his theoretical orientation, Edmondson finds the approach of *Therapeutic Discourse* unsatisfactory. The common-sense proposals for sequence at deep levels strike him as too informal and inexplicit; while he also suggests that no adequate description of conversation can be complete without a fully realized apparatus of surface sequencing rules (p. 61).

Edmondson also criticizes Labov and Fanshel for not sufficiently separating out two aspects of conversation which in his view are quite distinct. These aspects he refers to as the 'illocutionary' and the 'interactional': the illocutionary part of a description provides criteria for identifying utterances as illocutionary acts, while the interactional component contains the rules for sequencing units of conversation. Edmondson's major motivation in separating the two completely is one which we have already discussed: his etic approach to classifying illocutions dictates that the analyst avoid using contextual cues that are not available from the technical description of each act-type. As we pointed out earlier, this means discounting conversationalists' own perceptions of what their behaviour means and how it should be classified; it also means ignoring contextual information about what acts precede and follow the one you are analysing.

Of course, this information is considered indispensable by a number of analysts, including Labov and Fanshel. In *Spoken Discourse*, however, its use is strongly criticized: it can only vitiate the illocutionary classification. All too often, Edmondson alleges, the analysis of an utterance's illocutionary force is coloured by strictly interactional criteria, a remark tending to be analysed as a reply or acceptance, for instance, just where it follows a question or an offer—which is to say, exactly where one would expect an act of that type to be performed (pp. 59–60, 137–138). For Edmondson, each utterance has one illocutionary force and one only; furthermore, this must be recoverable without the use of interactional cues.

Is this distinction between illocution and interaction tenable? It seems that in making it, Edmondson is claiming that any sequence of utterances, such as the following (from our own data):

A_1 Andrew
B_1 Yes
A_2 Do you want some tea
B_2 Yes please
A_3 OK

has to be analysed *twice*: once for its illocutionary force (the intention with which each utterance was issued: for the text above this might go summons-answer-offer-acceptance-reply) and then again for the work each does in allowing interaction to proceed sequentially (for instance, we might want to specify that A_1 is an initiating move, that B_1 both closes the first pair sequence and opens the way for a new one, etc.). Language-users are alleged to be able to classify in two systems simultaneously (and independently). Edmondson comments:

> Slots in interactional structure are filled by units of behaviour: in the case of a conversational encounter, these units of behaviour will commonly be locutions having in their context of occurrence an illocutionary value (p. 114).

Yet part of any locution's 'context of occurrence' is precisely its position in ongoing discourse (something recognized by the Birmingham school and the ethnomethodologists to be considered in Chapters 4 and 6 below). This in turn suggests that illocution and interaction are not separate, but inter-dependent. One can argue this using the banal text above: what leads us to hear A_1 as a summons rather than say, an assertion about who killed Roger Ackroyd, is precisely its status in this instance as an initiating move.

If illocutionary force is a notion worth using in relation to conversation, it cannot be separated from interaction (and this means it is essential to go beyond the work of philosophers like Searle, who do not deal with connected discourse). It is absurd to claim that any utterance inherently possesses an illocutionary force, regardless of the context in which it is placed; and this presents problems for the kind of generalized rules so many analysts have sought to draw up for the interpretation of utterances as acts. There again, it must be recognized that conversation takes place in linear time, and as a rational human activity is therefore bound to be interpreted according to principles which take this into account (of Harris's (1981) notion of *cotemporality*). In the light of this observation we may suggest that sequence is not necessarily the arcane structural mystery it has sometimes been taken for. Nevertheless, it clearly does have a bearing on what act any utterance is construed as: otherwise it could be claimed that although the sequence

    Yes
    Andrew
    Yes please
    Do you want some tea

is odd *interactionally*, all the acts within it retain the same force as in the original, and are as easily interpreted as to their illocutionary value.

The interdependence of two different stages of analysis—classification and formulating rules of sequence—will be a theme of later chapters, especially Chapters 4 and 6, where surface sequential organization will be our most important concern. As far as speech act-based models are concerned, it seems sequence is rather a secondary preoccupation. The rules and units which are of primary importance are those relating to the classification of utterances as acts, an undertaking which constantly raises what we have dubbed the 'problem of intersubjectivity'. All the analysts whose work we have examined assume shared conventions, principles and rules: but as in the case of social psychology, no really convincing evidence is forthcoming in their work, and there are cogent reasons for doubting such assumptions.

From 'deep' to 'surface' analysis of conversation

We have tried to show that the use of the *illocutionary act* as a key theoretical concept in conversation analysis leads to a version of the rules and units model; and then to point out what difficulties and problems are raised by this particular version.

The illocutionary act is at bottom a *convention* whereby certain intentions of the speaker can be signalled. What conversation analysts who take it to be a fundamental unit in talk are claiming is that conversationalists share a whole series of these conventions, and are thus able to get, in Labov and Fanshel's phrase, 'from utterance to act'. There is a surface sequence of utterances: but on a deeper level there is 'what is really going on', and this entails that conversationalists share a knowledge of the acts which it is possible to perform, as well as the conventions by which they are performed.

In our analysis we have expressed serious doubts about this picture of communication. We have cited the work of Kreckel as evidence for scepticism on the issue of whether everyone agrees on the existence of a specific set of illocutionary acts, and specific conventions for performing them/interpreting them; we have also noted the difficulties that exist in actually formulating either a set of categories which are exhaustive, insightful and empirically satisfactory, or criteria for identifying tokens of such categories reliably.

The problem of classifying 'deep' illocutionary acts is such that many analysts have turned away from it, concerning themselves instead with more superficial patterning and with the hierarchical structure or 'grammar' of conversational interactions. One of the most influential models in this category is that produced by the so-called 'Birmingham school' of discourse analysis, whose approach is the subject of the next chapter.

4

Functionalism and Exchange Structure in Conversation Analysis

In considering the problem of sequential ordering as it arises in models using speech act theory, we touched on the subject of quasi-grammatical rules and their role in conversation analysis. The issues and problems which rules of this kind raise assume a central importance in the 'exchange structure' model which we consider in detail in the present chapter. Though in some ways it resembles the speech act approach (and has actually influenced Edmondson's model) the exchange structure model of conversation analysis is one of the most unreconstructedly 'grammatical', and therefore exemplifies a number of pitfalls in the rules and units framework with especial clarity.

The exchange structure approach is associated with a group of linguists (rather than psychologists or philosophers) who are frequently referred to as the 'Birmingham school'. Although not all of them work in Birmingham, their characteristic approach was developed during the 1970s in the English Language Research Group of Birmingham University; it has spread elsewhere as original group-members have found employment in various new locations, and also through the influence of publications outlining the methods and findings of the school.

The best-known representatives of the group are Malcolm Coulthard, J. McH. Sinclair, Martin Montgomery, Michael Stubbs and Michael McTear. Important associates include the systemicist Margaret Berry and the intonation specialist David Brazil (there is in fact a strong connexion between Birmingham discourse analysis and systemic-functional grammar, which is still an important paradigm in Britain). Many of the group have produced substantial work over the last ten years: Coulthard (1977) has written an introduction to discourse analysis, and so—more recently—has Stubbs (1983). They have also produced a collection of articles edited by Coulthard and Montgomery (1981).

As ever, our discussion of the Birmingham model will focus on its use of a rules and units framework, and on the related notion, developed especially by Stubbs, that it is possible to talk about 'discourse well-formedness'. It must at once be conceded that the Birmingham group has not produced a totally homogeneous body of work: there have been changes and developments with the passing of time, and there remain important differences between individuals. Yet by focusing on the themes of rules and units and well-formedness, we are confident we will be dealing with the major contribution this kind of analyis has made to the field.

Foundations of the Birmingham approach: toward grammars of talk

The 'grammatical' orientation and predilections of the Birmingham school can be seen clearly not only in their remarks on their own work, but also in their criticisms of other approaches. Reviewing a collection of ethnomethodological articles on conversation, Coulthard (1984) points out the informal, *ad hoc* character of much conversation analysis in the ethnomethodological paradigm, implying that this is not the kind of structural model he regards as helpful (though it is he concedes, *interesting*). A grammar of talk, according to Coulthard, would consist of 'a very small number of categories which are used to generate a very large number of structures'. There can be no *ad hoc* proliferation of categories to meet the varying demands of real data, if a model is to meet the rigorous standards by which a linguist would judge a grammar—the standards by which Coulthard clearly wishes to be measured. The same point is emphasized in Coulthard's early exposition of the model he and Sinclair developed to describe classroom interaction:

> We insist on a relatively small number of speech acts defined according to their function in the discourse and combining in predictable structures to form higher units (Sinclair and Coulthard, 1975, p. 11).

The use of the term *speech act* in the remark we have just quoted requires some comment, since it might be taken to imply that the Birmingham discourse model resembles Edmondson's in having a basis in speech act theory. Any such impression would however be misleading: although Sinclair and Coulthard are at pains to distinguish utterances in discourse from acts performed thereby, their conception of a speech act owes little to Searle or Austin. Instead of being defined by unvarying shared felicity conditions and by the intentions of the speaker, the acts which constitute conversation in the discourse analysis of Sinclair and Coulthard are 'defined by their function in the discourse'. This is an important clue to the theoretical underpinnings of the Birmingham model: essentially it is a form of *functionalism*, and is heavily influenced by the work of M. A. K. Halliday.

It is also a form of structuralism and distributionalism, rather in the manner of Harris or (especially) Pike, as can be seen from Sinclair and Coulthard's description of their framework:

> speech acts . . . combining in *predictable structures* to form *higher units* (p. 11, emphasis ours).

We are back in the domain of syntagmatic and paradigmatic relations, with hierarchically-ordered units and combinatory rules. How this orientation came about, and how it works in practical analytic terms, will be explained in more detail in the section which follows.

Origins and methods of the Birmingham approach

The foundations of the model now associated with the English Language Research group at Birmingham were laid in two research projects of the early 1970s: 'The English Used by Teachers and Pupils', which dealt with classroom interaction, and 'The Structure of Verbal Interaction in Selected Situations', which dealt mainly with doctor–patient interviews. A later project, 'The Structure of Lectures', attempted to solve the problem of monologue, which had suggested itself in the earlier work.

It is clear from the historical account given by Coulthard, Montgomery and Brazil (1981) that the researchers initially had a good deal of trouble developing a suitable analytic framework. They felt they were working in a total vacuum:

> when this project began a decade ago . . . there was virtually no relevant published research (Coulthard, Montgomery and Brazil, 1981, p. 1).

On the other hand, they took it as axiomatic that linguistic theory (i.e. syntax—they seem to have been unaware of the work of Pike (1967) and cite only Zellig Harris as an earlier discourse analyst) would be a source of illumination for their work. Clearly, when they began to analyse classroom interaction there were already very many approaches to that topic: the starting point for the Birmingham research was a belief that the powerful tools of linguistic theory could bring insights not available from existing approaches. Thus their model ultimately gave clear indications of having been adapted from grammatical description: specifically, it started out as a discourse version of Hallidayan scale and category grammar. As Fawcett has pointed out (1980, pp. 47–8), this places the model in the general category of 'slot and filler' approaches; and these are not new in the analysis of conversation, since Pike's Unified Theory (as Fawcett also notes) is an epitome of the 'slot and filler' type model. It is therefore not surprising that the Birmingham model raises many of the problems that Pike encountered, and which previous chapters have made all too familiar: segmentation, categorization and identification of tokens with types.

The study which established the Birmingham approach within the field of conversation analysis was Sinclair and Coulthard's *Towards an Analysis of Discourse*, which reported on the early research project, 'The English Used by Teachers and Pupils' (Sinclair and Coulthard, 1975). This study of a corpus of classroom interaction draws heavily on Halliday's Scale and Category Grammar, the early surface grammatical description which was later modified and extended to become the more familiar systemic-functional grammar (for readings on both these models and remarks on the development of Halliday's work, see Kress, 1976).

A scale and category grammar has three scales, *rank, exponence* and *delicacy*. The central structuring principle is the *rank scale*, defined as follows by Sinclair and Coulthard (1975, p. 20):

> The basic assumption of a rank scale is that a unit at a given rank, for example *word*, is made up of one or more units of the rank below, *morphemes*, and combines with other units at the same rank to make one unit at the rank above, *group*.

The descriptive problem is to determine how many ranks are needed to describe the data and where the rank scale stops: which units are themselves without structure (these mark the lower boundary) and which are incapable of combination to form further structures at the same level (these mark the upper boundary). The distinction between rank and level is an important one: although for Halliday morphemes are made of phonemes (to take an obvious example) these categories are related on the exponence scale, rather than being on the same rank scale. Phonemes expound morphemes, and there is thus a decisive break between phonology and grammar.

Sinclair and Coulthard make an important move when they argue that a decisive break like that between phonology and grammar also exists between grammar and discourse. Discourse is a new level. This argument is posed against the alternative conception, that units of grammar exist which are greater than the sentence (one possible candidate here is the paragraph, at least for written language), but which belong on the same rank scale as sentence and clause. This simple idea was in fact favoured by Harris: given a sound grammar of the sentence, discourse description must be more of the same (Harris, 1970, p. 374). Sinclair and Coulthard reject this on the grounds that

> Paragraphs have no grammatical structure; they consist of a series of sentences of any type in any order (1975, p. 20).

But if paragraphs and their spoken equivalent have no grammatical struc-ture, that is not to say they have no linguistic structure of any kind. Simply, it is a different sort of structure, requiring a move to a different level, from grammar to discourse, which has a new rank scale of its own.

It remains theoretically unclear why, if discourse is not just 'more of the same', it should necessarily be handled in the same way as grammar, that is, by means of a rank scale. There seems to be an implicit, and by no means logically inevitable claim here that discourse is like other levels in being segmentable and hierarchically structured. If it is an empirical claim only, it may be open to objections along the lines that (a) once nonverbal and paralinguistic behaviour is reintegrated with the data, segmentability becomes much more dubious (as Pike found); and conversely (b) if sufficiently broken down, any kind of human behaviour is trivially segmentable and perhaps even describable in terms of hierarchy (as Pike's work also demonstrates). Throughout the work of the Birmingham school, we discern an *a prioristic* determination to pursue analogies between discourse and grammar, however slim the evidence that parallels exist.

Apart from *level* and *rank*, the other concept which is important in Sinclair and Coulthard's approach is *function*, which is used in a way that differs slightly from the use of the term in Hallidayan functional grammar. For Halliday, function means something like, 'what this grammatical element is doing in a sentence; how syntactic choices carry implications in terms of transmitting a message, interacting with an addressee and creating a text.' For Sinclair and Coulthard on the other hand, function is a matter of organising the discourse, and has a sequential or distributional character:

> We are interested in the function of an utterance or part of an utterance in the discourse and thus the sort of questions we ask about an utterance are whether it is intended to evoke a response, whether it is a response itself, whether it is intended to mark a boundary in the discourse, and so on (Sinclair and Coulthard, 1975, p. 14).

It is this sort of distributional criterion that informs Sinclair and Coulthard's rank scale, which is as follows:

LESSON
TRANSACTION
EXCHANGE
MOVE
ACT

A stretch of discourse bounded by framing utterances such as *Right, OK, Now then*, which teachers use to mark a boundary in the lesson, is a TRANSACTION. It is composed of EXCHANGES: stretches that belong together because they evoke/respond to each other, as shown for instance by the directional arrows in the example below (Sinclair and Coulthard, 1975, p. 21, arrows added):

Teacher: Can you tell me, why do you eat all that food? [evokes response] →

Pupil: To keep you strong [is a response and evokes further response] ←→

Teacher: To keep you strong, yes, to keep you strong [is a response] ←

A move with no right-pointing arrow marks the closing of the exchange. The next utterance is not predicted by it, so that utterance will mark the opening of a new exchange. The move itself is the whole stretch to which an arrow applies, which need not be co-extensive with an utterance.

As well as being coded for its predictive/predicted status within an exchange, each move (and its component acts) is given a label such as 'elicit' or 'inform'. This sort of functional taxonomy can be drawn up for the units at each rank to produce a more 'delicate' classification. On the classification system as a whole, the following requirements are imposed (Sinclair and Coulthard, 1975, pp. 15–16): first, it must contain a finite number of classes; second, it must have clear, reliable criteria for exponence (i.e. it must be possible to decide, for any utterance, what class of move or act it instantiates); third, it must be comprehensive, that is, able to describe all the data; and fourth, there must be at least one impossible combination of symbols (i.e. sequential constraints on the structure of discourse, such that the ordering of classes is not random or free).

We can divide these requirements, and the problems they bring with them, into two main categories: the first three relate essentially to units, and raise the problems we have discussed in earlier chapters, namely segmentation, classification and the identification of tokens with types; while the fourth requirement relates specifically to the formulation of rules of sequence.

Because we have already examined the first set of problems in relation to a series of approaches to conversation, it might seem unnecessarily repetitious to discuss them again in any detail here. And indeed, we shall be paying more attention to the issue of rules and of the 'well-formed' discourse sequence. Nevertheless, the first three requirements of Sinclair and Coulthard's analytical framework will bear a certain amount of critical scrutiny. The 'grammatical' outlook of the Birmingham school dictates that the problems of segmentation, classification and type-token relations are solved within the model in particular ways, ways which recall the earlier expedients of linguistic analysts like Harris and Pike. Specifically, it is possible to discern in the model a leaning toward formal and distributional criteria.

Segmentation and classification: the problem of monologue

As we have observed, the Birmingham school began by analysing 'the English used by teachers and pupils', and it appears that this data presented few significant difficulties once the analytic framework had been constructed. Functional taxonomies work relatively well when they are designed for the description of a type of behaviour which is regular, highly structured and whose objectives are very well understood—as is the case with teaching exchanges in a school classroom. Unfortunately, other corpora of data proved less tractable.

The specific problem encountered by the group concerned the description of lengthy utterances and (*a fortiori*) monologic speech events; in a concerted attempt to tackle the problem, Coulthard and Montgomery undertook a project for the British Council on 'The structure of lectures' (reported in Coulthard, Montgomery and Brazil, 1981, pp. 31–39). The researchers already knew that functional taxonomies and rank scales were difficult to adapt to long utterances, in terms both of segmentation and classification:

> This is not to say that we were unable to perceive some structure but that we were unable to handle it within the model we were developing. The difficulty with trying to handle long moves as a *series* of informs was that we had no criteria for isolating the boundaries or for showing their relationship to each other (Coulthard *et al.*, 1981, p. 31).

The solution they adopt in the 'lectures' research is to set up a new rank scale, whose lowest rank, the MEMBER is defined syntactically (the next rank, SEQUENCE, seems to be defined by grammatical cohesion and only TRANSACTION, as in the classroom model, by framing boundaries). The more delicate description of MEMBER proves rather uninformative however:

> It is immediately apparent that the contribution is structured in terms of the points made and in broad terms this is signalled as the discourse unfolds by such surface markers as 'first', 'second', 'first of all', 'secondly' (Coulthard *et al.*, 1981, p. 32).

Later in the project it was found that

> the main discourse develops through a chain or succession of informing members. Although broadly they may be classed as informatives, they none the less enter into a variety of relationships with each other. Frequently they are linked together by a limited range of conjunctive items . . . thereby setting up chains of logical relations . . . three relationships in particular are seen as crucial: ADDITIVE, ADVER-

SATIVE, CAUSAL, and these correspond with . . . 'and', 'but' and 'so' (Coulthard *et al.*, 1981, p. 36).

Unable to think of obvious names for the parts of a monologue, Coulthard and Montgomery resort to counting and labelling the conjunctions: discourse units are once again to be defined by formalist criteria, and their boundaries fixed by the distribution of formal elements.

And what, in fact, does this analysis of the structure of lectures tell us? That lecturers habitually start at the beginning of their lectures, make a series of ordered remarks in the middle and finish at the end! As ever, the price of abolishing arbitrariness from a description (there is little argument about the presence or absence of conjunctions) turns out to be total banality and uninformativeness.

Type-token relations: from function to form

A similar resort to formalist criteria can be seen in relation to the recurring problem of identifying utterances as instances of particular acts. We have already observed that for the Birmingham school, function is not determined by conventional devices such as felicity conditions, nor is it defined by the intentions of the speaker. Rather, it is fixed by interactional and positional criteria, and this causes difficulties at the more delicate level of analysis. Here, utterances have to be classified less crudely than merely saying whether they initiate or respond; yet what they are really doing can be rather obscure, especially (once again) in types of interaction less regular and predictable than classroom analysis.

It is interesting therefore to see Birmingham analysts tending more and more to appeal to criteria about which there is unlikely to be any argument: the presence of conjunctions like *and, but* or *so*, and the incidence of particular prosodic features. For example, Coulthard *et al.* report on the findings of the project on doctor–patient interaction (1981). They identify a characteristic move whereby the doctor repeats part of a patient's utterance, e.g.

D: And how long have you had these for?
P: Well I had 'em er a week last Wednesday.
D: A week last Wednesday?

(Coulthard *et al.*, 1981, p. 20.)

However, they argue that this move has two possible functions, *elicitation*, where the doctor wants the patient to say more, and *follow-up*, where the doctor acknowledges that s/he has heard and assimilated the patient's remark.

The question then arises, how does the patient know which move the doctor is making when s/he repeats part of the patient's turn? For the patient it is quite an important decision, since whether the next turn is the doctor's or the patient's depends on whether the move is treated as follow-up or elicitation. According to Coulthard *et al.*, the criterion used by conversationalists at this point is prosodic: it lies in the *key* of the utterance. High key signals that the move is eliciting; low key signals a follow-up move.

But this solution raises familiar problems. How do the analysts actually know that conversationalists are using the prosodic criterion? What they have identified is an empirical regularity whereby high key utterances are usually followed by a response from the hearer: what they deduce from this is the existence of a rule or criterion for identifying two types of move. No further evidence is adduced for this conclusion, and nor is any explanation of it (i.e. how and why does high key signal eliciting moves? What is the connexion between the form and the function?). Using an objective, etic criterion like key makes analytic decisions about which move an utterance instantiates very easy; but to assume that the behaviour of conversationalists reflects or reproduces this procedure of analysis is a quite unwarranted leap of faith. To make good the assumption, the analyst must posit that conversationalists have 'tacit knowledge' of the descriptive generalization s/he formulates; which is then quite illegitimately transformed into a *prescription* which the speaker is said to be (tacitly) following. This sliding between 'prescriptive' and 'descriptive' rules is typical of quasi-grammatical approaches. The issue of what people tacitly know comes up again in the Birmingham model in relation to sequence and 'discourse well-formedness', the topic to which we now turn our attention.

Sequence, well-formedness and rules of discourse

It will be remembered that Sinclair and Coulthard laid down four requirements for an adequate discourse model. The first three related to classification, and the construction of taxonomies which were both finite and comprehensive, and whose classes had very clear criteria for exponence. The fourth, however, was rather different, as Sinclair and Coulthard themselves acknowledged: whereas the others

> could be general standards for linear string analysis . . . this one is linguistic (1975, p. 16).

The notion that not every combination of symbols is possible, or put another way that there should be some sequential constraint, is

> the basic notion of linguistic structure (p. 16).

What appears to be meant by this is that the 'at least one impossible combination of symbols' requirement is a constraint imposed on many formal syntactic descriptions within theoretical linguistics. We have already noted the propensity of Birmingham analysts to regard discourse and syntax as analogous levels of linguistic structure. The formal generative model of syntax impinges particularly on the Birmingham approach to the syntagmatic analysis of discourse (the sequential, as opposed to classificatory, part of the description); and since this is a topic we have touched on only briefly in previous chapters, we will focus on it here.

Rules

The requirement that an adequate discourse model include constraints on the distribution of units raises the whole question of what conversationalists might 'know' about producing orderly and coherent talk. If distributional regularities occur, with certain sequences being avoided by conversationalists (always supposing this is not just an artefact of the system used to classify sequence components), it is possible to hypothesize that participants in talk are governed by *rules* in putting conversations together. The analysts Michael Stubbs (1981, 1983) and Michael McTear (1981) have been notable proponents of this hypothesis.

Once again, the status of the rules is ambiguous as between description and prescription. Both Stubbs and McTear use forms of words which imply that the rules describe properties of discourse (rather than stating the norms on which speakers act). It is envisaged that analysts will formulate these rules as quasi-generative rewrite instructions, e.g.

E(xchange) → I(nitiation) R(esponse) F(eedback).

Stubbs remarks that the goal of discourse analysis is

to predict the surface distribution of forms (1981, p. 107).

Formulae of the type just given precisely specify the permissible distributions which the analyst expects to find in data—they capture, in other words, valid generalizations about acceptable and unacceptable sequences in talk. McTear is confident there are generalizations to be made:

It is not the case that any utterance can occur in combination with any other utterance . . . there are constraints on what items can follow what (McTear, 1981, p. 74).

Yet these generalizations, as it turns out, are not just statements about patterning in discourse; Stubbs and McTear make the (by now familiar) assumption that they must also describe what speakers tacitly *know*. Because a certain formulation such as

E → IRF

captures a generalization about regularities in classroom interaction, it is concluded that the formulation itself is being *followed* by participants to produce just this outcome. Regularities, in other words, are the consequence of rules.

An instance of the effortless move from descriptive 'is' to prescriptive 'ought' can be found in Sinclair and Coulthard's discussion of why teaching exchanges normally seem to have three slots—Initiation, Response and Feedback, as exemplified by the exchange from their data which we quoted on p. 70 above—whereas exchanges in other contexts usually have two. Sinclair and Coulthard state this regularity in the descriptive formula $E \rightarrow IRF$. But it is clear they attribute knowledge of this regularity in the discourse structure of teaching exchanges to competent participants in classroom talk, since they characterize the production of alternative sequences (such as $E \rightarrow IR$) as *deviant behaviour*:

> It is deviant to withhold feedback continually . . . thus the structure of (teaching exchanges) differs . . . in that F is a compulsory element (Sinclair and Coulthard, 1975, p. 51).

It is a rule of linguistic structure which participants in classroom talk 'know', that exchanges have three slots, whether or not three are filled (if they are not, the sequence is not unusual but *deviant*, a further indication that there is something structurally wrong with it).

Stubbs is aware that, strictly speaking, this view of what rules of discourse are leaves its proponents in the far from enviable position of having to find, for each rule they propose, some warrant in the actual behaviour of conversationalists. And he is also aware that this is very difficult if one confines oneself to looking at the discourse they produce. 'Deviant', bizarre and incoherent sequences are far from uncommon in discourse data: the literature of conversation analysis and text grammar is littered with attempts to construct 'impossible' sequences, but no sooner is a piece of 'discourse nonsense' proposed than some other analyst constructs a context in which it seems perfectly sensible and natural. Despite McTear's claim that not anything can follow anything (which on one level, after all, is a simple truism) it has not been possible to find an example of a categorical constraint on sequence which allows for prediction of what will come next.

Stubbs therefore retreats to the much weaker position embodied in the following comment (1981, p. 109):

> One way out of the problem is to switch from thinking about what might occur at any point in discourse to thinking about the interpretation of what does occur . . . we can maintain a useful distinction between competence (what speakers know about what can be expected to occur) and performance (what actually occurs).

This remark recalls the argument of Duncan and Fiske (see Chapter 2) that unexpected findings may be explained away as mere 'performance errors';

given the ubiquity of such 'errors' in natural conversation, it seems tantamount to saying that whereas conversationalists do not use their competence actually to produce discourse, they do use it to interpret the
incoherent sequences they have jointly produced as a result of this failure! In
any case, Stubbs's position here restates a principle familiar from generative
grammar: that 'tacit knowledge' may be displayed not in actual behaviour,
but in considered judgements ('intuitions') *about* behaviour. It is at this
point that Stubbs introduces the notion that conversationalists can make
judgements about 'discourse well-formedness'.

Well-formedness

The concept of well-formedness is borrowed from generative grammar,
and it is helpful to outline very briefly what it means before examining its
application to conversation.

It is a central assumption of Chomskyan linguistics that native speakers of
a language possess a 'linguistic competence' in virtue of which they can
recognize strings (sentences) produced by a grammar as either well-formed
or ill-formed. Given a sequence of English lexemes, such as

*up the stood on platform the a young man

speakers have clear intuitions that it is not a sentence of English. Even cases
which are not 'word salad', such as

*who did you see the woman that met yesterday

attract unambiguous judgements that they are ill-formed.

Stubbs wants to extend this type of judgement to sequences longer than a
sentence: specifically, to interactive discourse where each contribution is
perfectly well-formed as a grammatical sentence. Since any utterance in
conversation sets up expectations that must constrain the next speaker,
Stubbs reasons that there might come a point where native speakers will say
that a sequence of moves is 'not an exchange of the language'.

A judgement of that kind would be useful to the analyst as evidence for
hypothesized rules of discourse. Just as the Chomskyan 'motivates' rules of
syntax with reference to native speaker intuitions about whether a sentence
is grammatical or not, so Stubbs argues rules of conversation should be
motivated with reference to judgements by native conversationalists that
discourse sequences are either well- or ill-formed. If native conversationalists agree that some sequence is ill-formed, the sequential constraints laid
down by the analyst should contain a proscription of that particular
sequence: it is assumed that when the judges declared it ill-formed they
displayed tacit knowledge of this proscriptive rule.

The first question to be asked about all this is whether conversationalists do in fact have intuitions about discourse well-formedness. Stubbs does not see this as especially problematic: he maintains that such intuitions are regularly displayed in various types of conversational repair. Unlike the examples cited above of syntactic ill-formedness, examples of ill-formed discourse are quite common; but the fact they are queried and repaired shows indirectly that conversationalists have recognized their basic ill-formedness.

Stubbs gives an example to demonstrate his point (1981, p. 108):

A: I'm going to do some weeding.
B: Yes please.
A: What?
B: Yes please.
A: You don't listen to anything I say.
B: I thought you said you were going to pour some drinks.
A: No. I said I'm going to do some weeding.

Here, A's second utterance, *What*, marks her recognition of the preceding exchange (i.e. the first two turns) as ill-formed. Her third utterance, *You don't listen to anything I say*, confirms this. The exchange

I'm going to do some weeding.
Yes please.

for some reason fails to meet A's tacitly known criteria for a well-formed exchange of English conversation.

A problem that immediately arises here is how far we can take repair and only repair, as displaying intuitions that some exchange is 'ill-formed' (assuming for the sake of argument that we can actually recognize repairs in the first place—see Chapter 6 for a discussion of this issue). There are, presumably, a vast array of reasons why a speaker would choose to initiate repair, and these need not necessarily imply any structural oddity in the stretch being repaired (it could indicate, for instance, that the speaker had misheard; or that s/he couldn't understand, or couldn't believe, some proposition contained in the interlocutor's remark). There are also many reasons why someone might choose *not* to repair, or might fail to do so, even if a stretch appeared entirely ill-formed. All in all, then, there must be some uncertainty about which repairs indicate tacit knowledge of ill-formedness, and whether equally important items of tacit knowledge are not displayed in other ways, or perhaps not displayed at all. Furthermore, if we admit that this uncertainty exists, the project of inferring tacitly-known rules of discourse from judgements of well-formedness is to some extent vitiated.

But supposing we accept that in Stubbs's example, A's behaviour as the interaction develops is a sign that she takes as an ill-formed exchange the sequence *I'm going to do some weeding/Yes please*, we are faced with another very difficult problem, namely what is the basis for the judgement of ill-formedness? One possibility which Stubbs in fact recognizes is also an Achilles' heel for Chomskyan linguists: the speakers to whom this exchange is presented might turn out to have conflicting intuitions about it (he is careful to say that A 'heard' it as ill-formed, and that someone else might well have found it perfectly well-formed). In the Chomskyan paradigm, differing intuitions are often put down to the informants' possessing slightly different 'grammars' of tacitly-known rules. But especially where conversation is concerned, this begs the crucial general question of whether well- and ill-formedness are in the rules at all, or whether they are simply a function of the context.

For instance, it would surely be overstating the case to claim that *I'm going to do some weeding/Yes please* is ill-formed for all speakers of English on all possible occasions. It is perfectly possible to imagine situations where *I'm going to do some weeding* would be taken as an offer, or where *Yes please* in response to it would convey the speaker's enthusiasm that the weeding should be done. Moreover, there is plenty of evidence to suggest that conversationalists themselves try to imagine some framework in which exchanges they are engaged in will appear to be well-formed. Citing an announcement on Scottish radio,

> Today we have a discussion of vasectomy, and the winner of the do-it-yourself competition

Stubbs observes that

> given any two utterances in discourse, it is usually possible to relate them, even if they were not intended to be related (1981, p. 108).

But if this point is accepted as a truism, it only raises further problems about the validity of formulating structural rules proscribing certain sequences as 'ill-formed discourse'. If conversationalists were using a purely linguistic kind of knowledge about what sequences of moves or acts are 'well-formed', and what utterances instantiate those sequences, they should reject particular combinations on the grounds that 'what x just said wasn't a possible exponent of moves p or q, which were the only appropriate moves to make at that point'. In fact, as Stubbs himself notes, they strive to interpret the most unlikely contributions to talk as rational and appropriate.

The point we are making here can be illustrated using the rule of classroom discourse we cited earlier, that teaching exchanges have three slots not two, Initiation, Response and Feedback. In the words of Sinclair and Coulthard (1975, p. 74):

> F is a compulsory element . . . it is deviant to withhold feedback continually.

It may well be the case that participants in classroom talk do judge the withholding of feedback as 'deviant'. Yet where is the virtue in an account of this which regards that judgement as a product of knowledge about structural constraints? A teaching exchange without a feedback move is not bizarre in the way that word-salad is bizarre: it is 'deviant' because it undermines the understanding pupils have of what teachers are trying to accomplish through these exchanges. When the point of an exchange is for pupils to demonstrate that they know the one answer the teacher is looking for, withholding feedback when an answer has been given is a way of behaving which does not make sense. Perhaps, then, there are no well-formed and ill-formed discourse sequences, but only rational and non-rational discourse moves.

Stubbs is prepared to concede the importance of rationality and strategic factors, but he insists conversation is both rational *and* rule-governed. The rules are there, but they can be *used strategically*. If this suggestion is not entirely incoherent (and given the Birmingham analysts' concept of tacit knowledge and the tendency to confuse descriptive generalizations and followable prescriptions, their model in practice consisting only of the former, we would be prepared to argue that it *is* incoherent) it marks yet another instance of the breakdown of any analogy between discourse and syntax (for who would ever claim that speakers of English were 'using the subjacency principle strategically'?). The lack of parallel is assiduously documented by Stubbs himself (1983, Chapter 5): he makes a number of remarks to the effect that discourse rules are not much like rules at other levels. Rules in discourse always draw on extralinguistic knowledge, whereas rules elsewhere in language do not; discourse rules are subject to blatant and repeated violation, whereas syntactic and phonological rule-violation is almost never found in natural data; discourse rules can be used 'strategically' where rules of phonology and syntax cannot; and so on. If these points have any substance to them, it becomes necessary to ask in what sense one can talk about 'rules of discourse' at all.

As far as rationality and strategy are concerned, they certainly seem to be very necessary if Stubbs is to save the claims of exchange structure models to have anything to say about syntagmatic patterns. It would be extremely difficult to state rules for surface sequence in discourse *without* invoking highly contextualized notions of strategy; one certainly could not do it using the kinds of simple ordering restrictions on the kinds of classifications proposed by the Birmingham exchange-structure model. Indeed, they are all the more problematic because the classifications themselves often depend on prior notions of contextual strategy (for instance, our identifying certain utterances as *elicits* does not and cannot depend on form or on position within the discourse alone; it must also draw on our understanding of teaching strategy). But if this is accepted, it is simply not clear that surface sequence rules and the concept of well-formedness have any theoretical utility at all.

In Chapter 5 we examine an approach to conversation which explicitly rejects both quasi-grammatical rules of sequence and conventions of the type employed in speech-act based models. For conversation analysts of the 'Gricean' tendency, talk is not governed by these rules and conventions, but rather by the overarching general principles of human rationality and rational behaviour.

5

Gricean Pragmatics and Conversational Principles

Although our interests remain focused on the notions of the rules and units of conversational structure, it is not always easy to avoid widening that focus. In particular we are led to stray from our chosen domain of conversation analysis into the domain of pragmatics, the study of utterance interpretation. This is inevitable, for some concerns of pragmatics overlap with our interests in conversational rules and units and, as a result, have had considerable influence on the theories and methodologies proposed by conversation analysts.

One school of thought in pragmatics that has had a strong influence in conversation analysis is that which has its source in the work of H. Paul Grice. Within the Gricean perspective we may loosely group the work of Leech (1982), Levinson (1979), Brown and Levinson (1978), Lakoff (1977), Sadock (1978), Gazdar (1979), Lyons (1981), Sperber and Wilson (1986), and others. These analysts, even though they describe their work as pertaining to pragmatics, make use of the notion of conversational principles (or sometimes 'rhetorical' or 'pragmatic' principles). For this reason, their work will concern us here. Yet, because of our special interest in the issue of rules and units in conversation analysis, we will not consider their disagreements over the nature of utterance interpretation, the central topic in pragmatic study. To enter into the debates about the nature of utterance interpretation would mean leading this discussion far from the central concerns of this book. Instead, we will restrict our discussion of Gricean pragmatics to a consideration of the notions of conversational principles and maxims as alternatives to the notion of conversational rules. Some Griceans, in particular Leech (1983), have emphasized the differences between rules and conversational principles. It is these differences, and the advantages principles are held to provide in accounting for the orderliness of conversational behaviour, that will most concern us here.

Grice originally presented his theory of conversational principles, maxims and implicatures in his series of William James lectures at Harvard University in 1967. These have never been published in their entirety, although two portions of them have appeared as independent articles (Grice, 1975, 1978), and mimeograph copies of the lectures themselves have circulated widely. Together they have had considerable influence in conversation analysis, equal to that of Austin's own William James Lectures, in which he introduced the notion of the speech act.

Grice begins his discussion by pointing out that conversations are not made up of a series of disconnected remarks; rather, they are characteristically rational, co-operative events (Grice, 1975). He claims that the participants in a conversation will recognize a common purpose or set of purposes, which may evolve during the conversation and may be more or less definite.

> But at each stage, SOME possible conversational moves would be excluded as conversationally unsuitable. We might then formulate a rough general principle which participants will be expected (*ceteris paribus*) to observe, namely: Make your conversational contributions such as is required, at the stage at which it occurs, by the accepted purpose or direction of the talk exchange in which you are engaged (Grice, 1975, p. 45).

This general principle of conversational interaction, helping to organize participants' contributions around a common purpose, Grice refers to as the 'Co-operative Principle' (hereafter abbreviated as 'CP').

Grice goes on to identify a number of specific maxims and sub-maxims which fall under and jointly make up the force behind the CP. Our concern here is not with the specific selection of maxims and sub-maxims. Whether they should be reduced to one, as Sperber and Wilson argue, or whether they should be augmented by many more, as Leech and Brown and Levinson argue, their primary function remains fundamentally the same: that of constraining the participants' behaviour so as to make conversations orderly, purposeful, and maximally efficient. We will not dwell on the differences between specific proposals but will instead focus on a distinctive character of maxims and principles as normative constraints.

Grice suggests that there are nine maxims, which jointly support the Co-operative Principle. They are organized into four general categories.

1. Quantity
   i. Make your contribution as informative as is required (for the current purposes of the exchange).
   ii. Do not make your contribution more informative than is required.
2. Quality
   i. Do not say what you believe to be false.
   ii. Do not say that for which you lack adequate evidence.
3. Relation
   i. Be relevant.

4. Manner
    i. Avoid obscurity of expression.
    ii. Avoid ambiguity.
    iii. Be brief (avoid unnecessary prolixity).
    iv. Be orderly.

(Grice, 1975, p. 46).

Few commentators pause to consider Grice's avowed motive for introducing the CP. Instead they rush on to consider the various maxims which are subordinate to it. For it is when one or more of these maxims are violated that the hearer, in an attempt to preserve the assumntion that the speaker *is* still following the CP, will try to deduce some unstated proposition that the speaker may have wished to convey by flouting a maxim. This proposition Grice calls an 'implicature'. Thus Grice's theory provides an account of how an utterance may be interpreted as communicating more propositional knowledge than the literal meaning of its words and syntactic form would suggest. Grice illustrates his account with the following example.

    A. How is C getting on in his job at the bank?
    B. Oh quite well, I think: he likes his colleagues, and he hasn't been to prison yet.

(Adapted from Grice, 1975, p. 43.)

The reply given by B may seem to imply more than it may literally be taken to mean. For instance, it seems to suggest the proposition Q: working in a bank is a potentially risky job for C. But why does B's utterance imply (implicate) Q? Grice's answer is that by flouting the Maxim of Relation, B's reply leads the hearer to reason that if B may still be assumed to be observing the CP, then he must be taken as implying Q.

> In a suitable setting A might reason as follows: '(1) B has apparently violated the maxim "Be relevant" and so may be regarded as having flouted one of the maxims conjoining perspicuity, yet I have no reason to suppose that he is opting out from the operation of the CP; (2) given the circumstances, I can regard his irrelevance as only apparent if I suppose him to think that C is potentially dishonest; (3) B knows that I am capable of working out step (2). So B implicates that C is potentially dishonest' (Grice, 1975, p. 50).

By this reasoning, Grice provides pragmaticists with a means of working out how it is that utterances are often interpreted as meaning more than they actually may be taken to have said. Consequently, Grice's theory has assumed an important place in the study of pragmatics.

Leaving its relevance to questions of utterance interpretation to one side, Grice's proposals may also be, and have been, seen as of potential importance for the analysis of conversational structure. To see this we must return to consider Grice's avowed motive for introducing the CP. He refers to the observable orderliness and rationality of conversations to justify the CP.

> Our talk exchanges do not normally consist of a succession of discon-
> nected remarks, and would not be rational if they did. They are
> characteristically, to some degree at least, co-operative efforts; and
> each participant recognizes in them, to some extent, a common purpose
> or set of purposes, or at least a mutually accepted direction. (. . .) But at
> each stage, some possible conversational moves would be excluded as
> conversationally unsuitable (Grice, 1975, p. 45).

We may take Grice to be claiming that there must be something which
makes it that, at any particular moment in a conversation, some possible
moves are nevertheless unsuitable. Some principle (or rule, or constraint,
etc.) determines what would be suitable and what would not. It is this
perceived need for an explanation of the orderliness of conversational
sequences, an orderliness which facilitates the maximally efficient exchange
of information, which leads Grice to postulate the existence of a CP
governing conversational behaviour. Obviously, given such a rule, the Co-
operative Principle falls squarely within our own interests in the analysis of
conversational organization.

Having introduced the CP and its maxims, Grice then raises what he
claims to regard as

> a fundamental question about the CP and its attendant maxims,
> namely, what the basis is for the assumption we seem to make . . . that
> talkers will in general (*ceteris paribus* and in the absence of indications
> to the contrary) proceed in the manner that these principles prescribe
> (Grice, 1975, pp. 47–48).

It is important to distinguish between two issues. The first, already discussed
above, concerns Grice's reasons for proposing the CP and its maxims. He
suggests that it is the orderly and purposeful character of conversation
that motivates this proposal. The second issue, raised in the quote cited
above, concerns the reasons why speakers and hearers will behave in the
manner prescribed by the CP and its maxims. Whereas the first issue has
to do with the descriptive adequacy of Grice's principles and maxims,
the second concerns their normative force. He considers two possible
bases for the assumption made by conversationalists that their partners
will in general follow the CP. The justification of that assumption might
simply lie in experience and observation. That is, we might have come
to assume obedience of the CP on the part of our co-conversationalists, as
a result of our experience of countless conversations in which the participants, at the very least, behaved *as if* they were following the CP.
Grice calls this justification, which we may refer to as the 'empiricist's
motivation',

a dull but, no doubt at a certain level, adequate answer to the question posed above (Grice, 1975, p. 48).

The answer that Grice prefers to the empiricist's justification is one which relies on more general principles of human reasoning (call this the 'rationalist's motivation')

> I would like to be able to think of the standard type of conversational practice not merely as something that all or most do IN FACT follow but as something that is REASONABLE for us to follow, that we SHOULD NOT abandon (Grice, 1975, p. 48).

In other words, the conversationalist follows the CP, and may justifiably be assumed by his audience to follow the CP (*ceteris paribus*), because it conforms to principles of human rationality. It's not just a matter of habit, as the empiricist's justification seems to imply. Rather we are justified in assuming observance of the CP for the same reason that conversationalists are led to obey it: it's the rational thing to do. Grice offers the following characterization of the rationality involved.

> I would like to be able to show that observance of the CP and maxims is reasonable (rational) along the following lines: that anyone who cares about the goals that are central to conversation/communication (e.g. giving and receiving information, influencing and being influenced by others) must be expected to have an interest, given suitable circumstances, in participation in talk exchanges that will be profitable only on the assumption that they are conducted in general accordance with the CP and the maxims (Grice, 1975, p. 49).

In support of his claim that the CP and its maxims are based on more general principles of rationality, Grice notes that their prescriptions have analogues outside of conversational interaction. For instance, if you are helping me to repair my car, I expect your contributions to that joint endeavour to conform to the maxims of quantity. Should I need exactly four screws at a particular moment, I will expect you to provide four screws: no more, no less. Nor do I expect you 'out of the blue' to hand me a cookery book; that would violate the maxim of relevance. In other words, Grice seems to feel that the principles and maxims which he claims to govern conversational interaction are derived from more general principles of rational interaction. I conform my behaviour to the CP and its maxims and my audience will expect my behaviour so to conform simply because I am a rational human being who is not to be expected to perform irrationally unless there is a particular countervailing force.

In fact, Grice makes no more of an attempt to demonstrate the strength of his rationalist argument. Nevertheless, its truth has been assumed by many of those who work within the Gricean paradigm. The CP is seen not as an arbitrary convention or as a conditioned habit but rather as a natural, rational principle motivated by the desires and requirements imposed on any human agent interacting with another human. We do not enter into an agreement to follow the CP, nor do we enter into interaction with our fellow human beings. In this respect, Grice's CP is very different from the other rules, conventions, principles, and constraints that have been proposed by other conversation analysts. For they have generally been framed in conventionalist terms. Speech act conventions and other discourse rules are not generally presented as motivated by deeper, 'rational' principles, but are seen simply as arbitrary conventions of the society in which the interaction takes place. Rationalism is distinctive of the Gricean approach, although we shall see that it has had some influence within the ethnomethodological perspective on conversation analysis.

It is revealing to note that in the short history of conversation analysis there have been three basic ways of motivating a rule-based account of conversational organization: rationalism, conventionalism, and empiricism. Similarly, the same types of motivation have been invoked, in the history of grammar, to justify a rule-based account of grammatical structure. For instance, the rationalist *Grammaire générale et raisonée* of Arnauld and Lancelot argues that words may only be combined into sentences in certain ways because the concepts designated by those words may only be combined in certain ways into the thoughts for which sentences stand. The universal rules of grammar were thought to be determined by the rational laws for the formation of thoughts (Arnauld and Lancelot, 1660). For a conventionalist like Saussure, possibilities of syntagmatic combination were determined not by underlying reason, but by the arbitrary conventions of the linguistic community (Saussure, 1983). The empiricist grammarian does not argue for a rational or a conventional basis for grammatical rules. Rather they arise as a result of experience. For instance, A. H. Gardiner, one of the last linguistic theorists in the empiricist tradition, takes the word order patterns in a language to be the result of habits, learned through the repeated experience of similar patterns. I keep to those patterns not because they are rational or because I have entered into some sort of social contract, but because I have seen them used in countless occasions of successful speech (Gardiner, 1932, discussed in Taylor, 1987).

In conversation analysis we find the same divisions. The position of Searle, and of most of those who take the speech act to be the fundamental unit of conversational structure, is one of conventionalism; there is no reason—natural, logical, or other—why satisfaction of a given set of felicity conditions should result in the performance of some particular act. Grice and his followers, on the other hand, argue that conversational rules are not arbitrary and are not simply the products of social conventions. Rather, as we have seen, they are motivated by rational principles. The empiricist position Grice at first considers and then labels as a 'dull' though adequate answer. To our knowledge, although there are some strands of empiricism in many of the conversation theories, notably in ethnomethodology, it has only once been proposed to account for the organized nature of conversational interaction. This is, again, in *The Theory of Speech and Language* by Alan Gardiner (1932: see especially his account of 'the *modus operandi* of a simple act of speech', pp. 71ff.).

To avoid confusion, we ought perhaps to say how the functionalist orientation of conversation analysis relates to this tripartite division between rationalist, conventionalist, and empiricist accounts of the nature of conversational rules. All of the conversational models we have so far considered are functionalist, in that they see conversational organization as a functional structure designed for the performance of certain inter-actional tasks: issuing warnings, transmitting information, exchanging turns, persuading, being polite, promising, etc. They differ, however, in viewing the motivation behind the rules constraining that organization as having its source in rationality, in human agreement, or in experience and habit.

Although Grice's rationalism is clear, he does not support it at any length. Of those within the Gricean perspective, it is Leech (1983), Brown and Levinson (1978), and Sperber and Wilson (1986) who produce the most developed arguments in support of a rationalist motivation for conversational principles. Perhaps the most developed account is that of Sperber and Wilson (1986), although they abandon Grice's CP and maxims and replace them by a single Principle of Relevance. We will have more to say about this alternative later. Brown and Levinson, on the other hand, base their rationalism on Erving Goffman's notion of 'face'. They propose Grice-like principles of politeness which are rationally motivated by the desire to preserve face. As this view had had some degree of influence on the ethnomethodological accounts of preference ordering, we will postpone discussion of it until the next chapter. Instead we will focus our remaining discussion in this chapter on the rationalist argument produced in Geoffrey Leech's *Principles of Pragmatics*.

> The rules of grammar are fundamentally conventional; the principles of pragmatics are fundamentally non-conventional, i.e. motivated in terms of conversational goals (Leech, 1983, p. 24).

Geoffrey Leech's *Principles of Pragmatics* is the fullest and most explicit development of Gricean ideas yet published. Leech is aware of the potential of much of what Grice himself only implies, and in the *Principles of Pragmatics* he produces an explicit account and expansion of the Gricean position. His aim is to present a new framework for conceptualizing the relations between language and language-use. This involves a principled distinction between grammar, the study of language, and pragmatics, the study of language-use. Whereas language is seen as rule-governed, language-use is seen as principle-controlled (Leech, 1983, p. 21), in the sense of Gricean principles and maxims. Consequently, in his effort to explicate his conception of the field of pragmatics, Leech discusses at length the nature of conversational principles, distinguishing them in particular from grammatical rules.

For Leech, conversation is best explained as a goal-directed activity, consisting in the implementation of interactional strategies. The participants will have various illocutionary goals, and they will design their utterances as strategies for the attainment of those goals. I may want to warn you about your friend's mood, so I choose a strategy which, when behaviourally realized, should bring off that warning: e.g. I say 'Watch out, she's angry!' Other behavioural strings could also have fulfilled that strategy and thus succeeded in attaining my goal of warning you.

At the same time, Leech sees conversational strategies as designed with the aim of achieving other goals besides illocutionary goals. One such goal would be the observance of the Co-operative Principle, a goal which as we have seen in your discussion of Grice, is itself motivated by the desired purpose of conversation: the maximally effective exchange of information (Grice, 1975, p. 47). Another such general goal would be the observance of what Leech calls the 'Politeness Principle' (or simply PP). The PP is motivated by the desire

> to maintain the social equilibrium and the friendly relations which enable us to assume that our interlocutors are being cooperative in the first place (Leech, 1983, p. 82).

Leech proposes other conversational principles (or 'rhetorical' or 'pragmatic' principles: the terms appear to be interchangeable). These, along with a host of supplementary maxims and submaxims allow Leech to develop a rhetorical model of language-use: i.e. a model based on

> a set of conversational principles which are related by their functions (Leech, 1983, p. 15). The rhetorical principles socially constrain communicative behaviour in various ways but they do not (except in the case of 'purely social' utterances such as greetings and thanks) provide the main motivation for talking. Cooperation and politeness, for instance, are largely regulative factors which ensure that, once conversation is under way, it will not follow a fruitless or disruptive path. It is therefore necessary to distinguish between illocutionary goals and special goals . . . (Leech, 1983, pp. 16–17).

Leech offers the following diagram as an illustration of his interpretation of conversational acts as goal-directed.

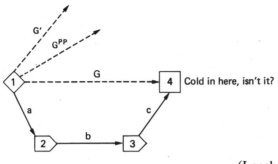

(Leech, 1983, p. 38)

Here, box 1 is supposed to represent the initial state of the interaction: the speaker feels cold. Box 2 stands for the first intermediate state: the hearer understands that the speaker is aware of the cold. The box labelled 3 represents the second intermediate state: the hearer realizes that the speaker would like the heater to be turned on. Box 4 is the final state: the heater is turned on and the speaker begins to feel warm. The lower-case letters a, b and c stand for particular actions. The speaker's action of remarking the cold is a. The hearer's action of inferring that the speaker wants the hearer to turn on the heater is b. And c is the hearer's action of turning on the heater. Finally, three goals are identified. G^{PP} represents the goal of observing the Politeness Principle. G' represents unspecified additional goals which the speaker may have in speaking (e.g. seeing if the hearer knows how to turn the heater on). G itself is the illocutionary goal of attaining state 3, i.e. getting warm. The goal of observing the CP would presumably be included under G' (Leech, 1983, p. 38). The speaker could have accomplished G (the goal of getting warm) by any one of a variety of means. These would include saying other sentences in place of 'Cold in here, isn't it?' For instance, he could simply have said 'Turn the heater on', or 'Get me warm', or 'Did you turn the heater off on purpose?', etc. But according to Leech's account, because of the speaker's social goal of upholding the Politeness Principle and other rhetorical principles, he was led to choose this way of attempting to attain goal G. For by being indirect and by avoiding the issuance of a direct command he can attain his illocutionary goal without being impolite, thus observing the Politeness Principle.

It must be taken as a general principle of goal-directed behaviour that individuals adopt the most direct course of action that is judged to be consistent with the fulfillment of their goals (. . .). Hence if an s (a speaker) . . . employs an indirect strategy to fulfil a goal in addition to

G, this is the justification for positing the extra goal G^{PP} of preserving the Politeness Principle (PP), and thereby maintaining good social relations. The CP, the PP, and other rhetorical principles may, in this analysis, be seen as regulative goals which persist as part of the background against which all other goals must be considered. (. . .) Other goals may conflict or compete with these goals, and most obviously, an impositive goal (one requiring imposition of one's will on someone else) runs counter to the principle of politeness. Thus the making of an 'innocent', non-impositive remark such as *Cold in here, isn't it?* becomes a gambit for reconciling competing goals . . . (Leech, 1983, p. 40).

In fact, we might interpret the utterance 'Cold in here, isn't it?' as an example of a case where the Politeness Principle and the Co-operative Principle constitute conflicting goals, with the utterance chosen providing an effective compromise. For if the speaker were to obey all the maxims which make up the CP, he simply would have said something like 'Turn on the heater so that I may become warm.' But this would have gone against the Politeness Principle (or, to be exact, its subsidiary Tact Maxim: 'Minimize the cost to the hearer'). Instead, by overtly remarking on the temperature, the speaker is able to obey the PP, although sacrificing complete obedience of the CP, in order to let the hearer infer the action that he should perform, rather than have it be commanded of him.

It is worth noting here that one of the motivations for proposing the Politeness Principle seems to be that, if we take its observance to be an important normative goal, then we can more easily account for the countless conversational utterances which appear to violate the CP or one of its maxims. This method of explaining away violations of the CP is overtly adopted by Brown and Levinson (1978) in their account of the production of politeness phenomena and its relation to the desire to avoid or mitigate face-threatening acts. They take Grice's maxims to apply to every conversational exchange but point out that

> . . . this does not imply that utterances in general, or even reasonably frequently, must meet these conditions, as critics of Grice have sometimes thought. (. . .) The whole thrust of this paper is that one powerful and pervasive motive for *not* talking maxim-wise is the desire to give some attention to face. (. . .) Politeness is then a major source of deviation from such rational efficiency, and is communicated precisely by that deviation (Brown and Levinson, 1978, p. 100).

Leech cites another example, reportedly uttered by an American hostage in Iran just before his release.

Considering that I am a hostage, I should say that I have been treated
fairly (Leech, 1983, p. 23).

This example is used to illustrate the multi-functionality of an utterance:
that is, the way it is strategically designed to accomplish a number of possibly
conflicting goals at the same time. Leech assumes that the speaker here is
trying to provide something useful to the reporters who had asked about his
treatment, to reassure the American public as well as his own family, to tell
the truth, and to avoid angering his Iranian captors by saying something
offensive to them (and thus delaying his own release) (Leech, 1983, p. 23).
Leech argues that such an example illustrates the absurdity of the practice of
classifying utterances as the performance of a single type of act: e.g.
'declaring', 'reporting', etc. On the contrary, the utterance above can be
taken as performing a variety of acts or as attempting simultaneously to
accomplish a number of goals.

> A better model might be something nearer to a linguistic juggling act, in
> which the performer has to simultaneously keep several balls in the air:
> to fulfil a number of goals which compete with one another. Of these
> goals, obeying the CP (giving the required amount of information,
> telling the truth, speaking relevantly) must be considered only a part
> (Leech, 1983, p. 23).

It is difficult to quarrel with the general point that, in speaking, speakers
often have a variety of different aims. We might add that hearers also often
perceive a number of different points being made by a single utterance. One
can imagine the variety of interpretations which the news media derived
from the hostage's utterance quoted above, not to mention the interpretations possibly derived by his family, by the CIA, by his Iranian captors, and
so on.

Yet, while it is all very well to dismiss pragmatic theories which take every
utterance to perform a single act or to be aimed for a single goal, it is no
easier to identify a set of such acts or goals. On what grounds or with what
criteria would such a set be identified? Obviously, we are here straying into
the central domain of pragmatics, i.e. into the question of utterance
interpretation. But we do so only to uncover Leech's response to the
question of the conversational goals which a speaker may be said to have.
For Leech takes the goals of obeying the CP, the PP, and the other rhetorical
principles to be general conversational norms. Speakers are held to have
observance of the rhetorical principles as constant goal. It is only the
illocutionary goals, which vary from utterance to utterance. Consequently,
as far as rhetorical principles are concerned, there is not, in fact, any
problem determining if they are motivating the strategy behind a particular
utterance. For they always do so.

However, although this argument may seem to avoid the problem of identifying the rhetorical principles motivating an utterance (while leaving the problem of identifying the illocutionary goals), in fact it only shifts the identification problem to a more general level. For we still need to justify the claim that any particular principle is a constant goal of conversational interaction. Why should we accept the general claim that speakers design conversational utterances so as, for example, to maximize dispraise of self (the Modesty Maxim: Leech, 1983, p. 132), or to refrain from saying that for which they lack adequate evidence (the second Quality Maxim: Grice, 1975, p. 46)? The observance of these maxims is supposed to be one of the normative goals of conversational behaviour; yet no general justification is provided to support that claim. And any justification that is based on the empirical analysis of individual utterances runs up against the same identificational problem that Leech's general argument, as we have seen, was designed to avoid. If it is difficult to identify individual cases where such maxims provide conversational goals, should it be any easier to prove that they always do so?

A number of different frameworks have been proposed within the Gricean approach: everything from Sperber and Wilson's single overarching Principle of Relevance to the unlimited number of principles, maxims, and submaxims proposed by Leech. While it is difficult to choose between them on purely theoretical grounds, one would expect their adequacy to be best tested against empirical analysis of individual utterances. But it is just this sort of analysis that the rationalist orientation of the Gricean approach is designed to avoid. However, until one of the Griceans motivates their choice of maxims and principles by means of an empirical analysis of particular conversational events, we will be unable to evaluate the cogency of their competing proposals. It seems, then, that the rationalism inherent to the Gricean perspective results in making it difficult, perhaps impossible, to evaluate alternative proposals within that framework; for any evaluation will depend on the view taken of the nature of rationality.

We have seen, then, that rhetorical principles, for Leech, are not only motivated by higher principles of rationality; in turn, they also motivate the strategic production of conversational behaviour. That is, the strategies effected by conversationalists are influenced by their concern to observe certain rhetorical principles which are themselves said to be motivated by human rationality. Human interaction is goal-directed, and rational principles such as the CP and the PP arise and are observed because human agents recognise that their interactional goals can only be obtained if, to some extent, they co-operate with their interactional partners and give them every reason to return that co-operation. By thus inserting his own framework of principles and maxims within an expanded account of conversation as a goal-directed activity, Leech extends the model founded on Grice's rationalist concept of conversational principles.

Leech discusses a number of further differences between principles and rules.

> The kind of constraint on linguistic behaviour exemplified by Grice's CP differs from the kind of rule normally formulated in linguistics, or for that matter, in logic, in a number of ways. (. . .)
> (a) Principles/maxims apply variably to different contexts of language use.
> (b) Principles/maxims apply in variable degrees, rather than in an all-or-nothing way.
> (c) Principles/maxims can conflict with one another.
> (d) Principles/maxims can be contravened without abnegation of the kind of activity they control.   (Leech, 1983, p. 8.)

We have already seen an illustration of the point made in (c). It is not always possible, given certain illocutionary goals, to be both co-operative and polite. Thus in saying 'Cold in here, isn't it?' a speaker might be sacrificing full observance of the CP and its Quantity Maxim in order to avoid transgressing the Politeness Principle.

Points (a) and (b) refer to what we might call the 'flexibility' of principles compared to rules. In certain contexts it may seem more important than in other contexts that what you say be taken as polite: e.g. in talking to one's prospective in-laws. Furthermore, politeness, relevance, brevity, tact, and many of the other concepts to which the principles refer, are gradeable rather than all-or-nothing. There is a continuum of degrees of relevance, for instance, between the extremes of the completely irrelevant and the completely relevant. However, with regard to rules, there is no such continuum, in theory, between the grammatical and the ungrammatical. Agreeing subject and verb in person and number is grammatical, according to the English rule; not doing so is ungrammatical. The rule permits no middle options of semi-grammaticality. Nor does its applicability vary according to the context.

This naturally means that it is even harder to verify or falsify the general claim that there are conversational principles which we follow in producing conversational speech. For any potentially falsifying example can always be 'explained away' by saying that the speaker may believe himself to be speaking in a context where the relevant principle does not apply, or in which it applies only to a negligible degree.

Point (d) may be rephrased as stating that, while grammatical rules are constitutive, conversational principles and maxims are regulative. Producing a string of English words which is not in accord with the rules of English grammar amounts to failing to produce an English sentence. The rules of English are said to *define* what counts as an English sentence, whereas the conversational principles do not define what counts as a conversation. They merely serve as regulative constraints on conversational behaviour, but constraints that may be ignored without resulting in a failure to produce a conversational act. Even if I do not fully observe the politeness principle when I speak to you, nevertheless we will still have a conversation.

Related to this characteristic of conversational principles is a further characterisic which, Leech admits, has been 'carefully omitted from the above definition'. Still, he affirms its importance in distinguishing principles from rules. Principles have a normative character which, in some cases, makes them akin to moral imperatives. It worries Leech to refer to values and prescriptions in what he intends to be a scientific description of the principles of language use, but he admits that he cannot escape the prescriptive and value-laden nature of those principles.

> In saying that people normally follow the CP, then, one is by no means taking a moral stance. But one thing that cannot be denied is that principles introduce communicative values, such as truthfulness, into the study of language. Traditionally, linguists have avoided referring to such values, feeling that they undermine one's claims for objectivity. But so long as the values we consider are ones we suppose, on empirical grounds to be operative in society, rather than ones we impose on society, then there is no reason to exclude them from our inquiry (Leech, 1983, pp. 9–10).

It is interesting that both Leech and Grice express the conversational principles not as statements but as commands ('Be brief', 'Avoid ambiguity', etc.). Unlike statements, the form usually taken by grammatical rules ('Adjectives agree in gender with their nouns'), commands suggest a speaker who (a) is issuing the command and (b) has the authority to do so (or claims to have the authority). Orders do not normally come off unless someone who has the required authority has actually issued the order. Yet it is difficult to see who or what is intended as responsible for, for example, the command formulated as the CP:

> Make your conversational contribution such as is required, at the stage at which it occurs, by the accepted purpose or direction of the talk exchange in which you are engaged (Grice, 1975, p. 45).

Neither Grice nor Leech consider this issue, and yet it is important to the conceptual coherence of the notion of a conversational principle. Should we assume that society itself is the source of such prescriptions? If so, it needs to be explained in what way 'society' (whatever that means) can issue commands. Or are the commands thought to be issued by the individual conversational participants to themselves? Or is the answer that participants only act *as if* they were following commands issued by someone or something with the requisite authority, even though in truth no such issuant exists? Yet this would amount to saying that conversationalists do *not* in fact follow the commands listed as conversational principles because no such commands have in truth been issued. At the same time, we should also want to ask why the particular set of principles identified by Leech and Grice, rather than some other set, should be taken as the very set that each and every conversationalist is acting as if they were following.

In other words, for Gricean principles to make some sort of sense they have to be taken as issued by an authoritative force. Otherwise, they amount to no more than general descriptions of conversational behaviour, in which case their imperative formulation is bizarre. If we are to conceive of speakers and hearers as actually *following* the commands contained in the principles, then we require some person or some institution with the necessary authority to have issued those commands. To say that my behaviour is such that it is only *as if* it were guided by a particular principle amounts to the admission that I am not in fact following that principle. In this case it makes little sense to discuss the exact nature of such principles, how they differ from rules, how they apply various contexts, and how they may conflict with one another. We might as well debate the anatomical features of mythical beasts.

Given this discussion of the conceptual confusion incorporated in the Gricean notion of conversational principles, it is interesting to note that, in their book *Relevance: Communication and Cognition*, D. Sperber and D. Wilson, two early proponents of the Gricean perspective in pragmatics, come both to replace Grice's framework of principles and maxims by one overarching Principle of Relevance and abandon the formulation of principles in terms of prescriptive norms as well. They point out that Grice's principles and maxims are pictured as

> norms which communicators and audience must know in order to communicate adequately (Sperber and Wilson, 1986, p. 161).

However, they argue, conversationalists do not in fact really follow the CP and its maxims.

> It seems to us to be a matter of common experience that the degree of cooperation described by Grice is not automatically expected of communicators. People who don't give us all the information we wish they would, and don't answer our questions as well as they could, are no doubt much to blame, but not for violating principles of communication (Sperber and Wilson, 1986, p. 162).

Sperber and Wilson's alternative, the Principle of Relevance, eschews the prescriptive and normative quality of standard Gricean principles. Instead, it is presented as a descriptive generalization about the nature of conversational communication. It is not an imperative which communicators are thought to follow, or to act as if they were following. Indeed they do not even have tacit knowledge of the Principle of Relevance.

> The principle of relevance, by contrast, is a generalization about ostensive-inferential communication. Communicators and audience need no more know the principle of relevance to communicate than they need to know the principles of genetics to reproduce. Communicators do not 'follow' the principle of relevance; and they could not violate it even if they wanted to (Sperber and Wilson, 1986, p. 162).

It is interesting that Sperber and Wilson have abandoned the distinctive Gricean concept of normative principles in favour of a concept which is closer to the sort of descriptive generalization which it is the aim of social psychologists such as Duncan and Fiske to produce. No claim is made (or at least no claim *should* be made) that actors take such generalizations to be followable prescriptions. (On this distinction, see Chapter 1 above.)

However, as we have already seen, a different sort of problem arises with the interpretation of conversational principles as descriptive generalizations. In Sperber and Wilson's case, this problem may be seen in the ambiguous way they treat the notion of a principle. For they do not make it clear whether their Principle of Relevance is claimed to *cause* the regularities observed in conversational interaction (as we might assume the principles of genetics to cause certain genetic phenomena) or whether the Principle of Relevance is really a scientist's construct which only *describes* the relevant regularities. If the latter is the case (and they give no evidence or argument for the former), then we have not solved the riddle of the observable orderliness of conversational interaction. A description of that orderliness tells us nothing about why conversationalists behave in such a way as to produce it in conversation after conversation.

We thus find ourselves neatly situated in the central dilemma about rules (principles, maxims, norms, . . .) of conversation. To explain the apparent organizational aspects of conversational interaction we require more than a descriptive generalization which merely reformulates observable regularities. And yet by what method can we identify the rules which really generate those regularities, the rules which conversational participants may be shown actually to follow in producing conversations? The Gricean approach seeks to answer the latter question by postulating a list of deductive principles which conversationalists act as if they observe. But to say it is as if they were observing those principles is thereby to admit their fictional status. As a result such an approach dissolves either into a mythology inhabited by fictional rules, whose validity or explanatory value cannot be tested or falsified, or into descriptive generalization, the unsatisfactory position which the Gricean perspective was designed to replace.

This dilemma has been recognized and understood by those conversation analysts who are inspired by the work of the ethnomethodologist Harold Garfinkel. Their work may be seen as a persistent effort to escape the horns of the 'rules dilemma' and to identify the norms that conversationalists themselves follow in producing the observable orderliness of conversational interaction. In so doing, the ethnomethodologists have focused on improving the investigation of normative authority, of the ways in which rules may be said to be known to actors, and of the means by which rules constrain the behaviour of actors. The result has been a perspective which threatens to offer an alternative to the rationalist, conventionalist, and empiricist conversation theories thus far encountered. The following chapter will consider some aspects of their approach and of their proposed methodology for conversation analysis.

6

Ethnomethodology and Conversation Analysis

Like the discourse analysts discussed in Chapter 4, ethnomethodological conversation analysts form an identifiable 'school' whose approach is distinctive among the various approaches to conversation. The field, now often referred to simply as CA (a procedure we will adopt in this chapter), has an interesting and complex history, knowledge of which is essential to understanding its current concerns and methods.

Introduction and Historical Background

The history in question differs in almost every particular from that of the Birmingham discourse analysis school. CA originates outside the British tradition (in the USA) and outside linguistics (in sociology). Significantly, CA developed out of a break-away school of sociology, called 'ethnomethodology', which was not at first particularly concerned with conversational speech. Indeed, its original importance was as a theoretical and methodological critique of the established forms of sociology. In a recent book-length study (Heritage, 1984a) of the works of Harold Garfinkel, the American founder of the ethnomethodological school, ethnomethodology is said to have originated as a synthesis (and, at the same time, a critique) of the opposing sociological perspectives of Talcott Parsons and Alfred Schutz. The figure of Garfinkel still looms very large in CA, although his name is mentioned only rarely in CA publications of the past ten years. But it was Garfinkel, along with his graduate students, who first worked out the theoretical principles which today remain the essential pillars of the CA approach. Indeed, it is an undeniable although rarely acknowledged fact that, shorn of its ethnomethodological underpinning, CA would be almost indistinguishable from such orthodox models of conversation as that of Edmondson, Stubbs or Coulthard. It is Garfinkelian principles which give life to the distinctive methodology characteristic of CA. Although in recent years some of its practitioners have attempted to distance themselves from any association with Garfinkel, picturing CA as an atheoretical, inductive, autonomous method of analysis, it will be our argument in this chapter that the many strengths of CA, as well as its weaknesses, are to be attributed to the original Garfinkelian principles on which CA is founded. What those ethnomethodologists who now simply call themselves 'conversation analysts' have accomplished is an extended application of the original ethnomethodological methods to the study of a particular analytical domain: conversational interaction. But their findings should not, and indeed cannot fairly be treated as the fruits of an autonomous research programme.

It is worthy of note that, in 1984, a comprehensive study of Garfinkel, ethnomethodology and CA appeared in which the author also argues, as we do, that CA is a continuous development from Garfinkel's original ethnomethodological principles. This is John Heritage's *Garfinkel and Ethnomethodology* (1984a), to which we would refer any reader who wanted to learn more about the ethnomethodological principles behind CA and from whom we have drawn some of our examples. The reader will soon note that although we are in agreement with Heritage on foundational principles, we take a different view of the success CA has had in applying those principles in practice. We would also refer the reader to the chapter on CA in Stephen Levinson's *Pragmatics*, on which we have also relied as a source of examples and ideas.

Given these presuppositions, our treatment of ethnomethodological CA will begin with a brief sketch of the general principles of the ethnomethodological perspective in the study of social behaviour. This sketch will focus on the central principles of 'accountability', 'normativity' and 'intersubjectivity' and will try to locate the position of CA as an ethnomethodological domain with specific reference to its claim to an empirical methodology. Following this, we will provide a selective sketch of some of the principal results of the ethnomethodological study of conversation, i.e. of what the conversation analysts claim to have discovered as a result of this methodology. Then, we will consider the distinctive approach adopted within this methodology to the tasks of identifying units of conversational behaviour and of explaining the relations between these units. This section will be concerned to show both how those two essential methodological tasks are entirely indebted to ethnomethodological principles and how, in spite of considerable advantages over competing methodologies, many of the by-now-familiar problems remain unsolved.

According to remarks made at a conference in 1968 (reported in Garfinkel, 1974) the term 'ethnomethodology' arose out of Garfinkel's involvement in a research project in the late 1940s examining the behaviour of jurors. Garfinkel felt that the jurors were 'doing methodology' in the sense of managing their deliberations in accordance with certain notions of adequate evidence, reasonable accounting, etc. But this 'methodology' was done from a stand-point of commonsense rather than from expert legal knowledge. Therefore Garfinkel labelled it 'ethnomethodology', i.e. a social actor's, or a community's, own lay methodology. As he puts it, ethnomethodology

> . . . is an organizational study of a member's own knowledge of his ordinary affairs, of his own organized enterprises, where this knowledge is treated . . . as part of the same setting that it also makes orderable (Garfinkel, 1974, p. 18).

Ethnomethodology thus views 'practical reasoning' activities as being managed by social actors ('members') who strive to produce what they and others in the community will recognize as orderliness in those activities. The focus of interest for the researcher is therefore not only or simply the kind of orderliness any activity displays; rather, it is the (presumably shared) 'methods' or 'procedures' required to produce that orderliness. Garfinkel, like many other students of interaction, uses a 'dramaturgical' analogy: instead of describing the play, one describes the backstage activity that enables the play to be produced. It is this attention to 'backstage' phenomena (often described by ethnomethodologists as 'seen-but-unnoticed' by the participants: i.e. tacitly known) that differentiates the analyst from any ordinary, participating member; the analyst, as a competent social actor, is as capable as anyone of understanding and describing the play, but must in addition undertake

> an examination of the ways in which tacit rules and common sense theories were used by members in accomplishing the orderliness of particular settings (Atkinson and Drew, 1979, pp. 21–22).

The activity being managed by members is often very familiar and even banal. But as Garfinkel points out, the familiarity of an activity can breed 'contempt', in the sense of rendering its complex and managed character invisible ('seen-but-unnoticed'). The analyst is thus obliged to

> pose as problematic how utterances come off as recognizable unit activities. This requires the sociologist to explicate the resources he shares with participants in making sense of utterances in a stretch of talk. At every step of the way, inevitably, the sociologist will continue to employ his socialized competence, while continuing to make explicit what these resources are and how he employs them (Turner, 1974, p. 205).

As such, ethnomethodology might seem little different from many of the currently popular models of human action which assume that actors share tacit knowledge of a system of rules which they apply in regulating their behaviour. Most of the models of conversation we have so far discussed make similar assumptions, as do the leading schools of modern linguistics. But to assimilate ethnomethodology to these standard views of human action would be to misunderstand the very essence of the Garfinkelian principles on which ethnomethodology was founded, especially the crucial concepts of accountability and the architecture of intersubjectivity.

Accountability and the Architecture of Intersubjectivity

It is perhaps easiest to explain what is distinctive about the ethnomethodological notion of the 'practical reasoning' which underlies human behaviour by comparing it with the deterministic model it was designed to rebut. (For present purposes, we may here take to be deterministic not only Parsonian sociology—the original target of Garfinkel's attacks—but also structural and generative linguistics as well as the conversation analytic models of the Birmingham School, Edmondson, Clarke, and Duncan and Fiske.) Whereas the determinist says that the actor's behaviour is governed by rules which the actor has 'internalized', the ethnomethodologist does not view rules as governing the actor's behaviour in such a deterministic fashion. Rather, the ethnomethodologist takes actors to design their behaviour with an awareness of its 'accountability'. That is to say, aware of the rule relevant to the situation in which they find themselves, they choose to follow (or not to follow) the rule in the light of what they expect the interactional consequences of that choice to be. For they assume that their co-interactants also know the rule and will be judging their behaviour accountable for its conformity or non-conformity to the relevant rule. Ordinarily, the relevant rules will be followed; but when they are not followed, the co-interactants can be expected to look for the reasons why (is the actor angry? sloppy? inattentive? making a point?). Thus rules are conformed with, not because they determine behaviour, but because actors are generally aware of the consequences (e.g. the implications that will be drawn) of non-conformity. That is, they are aware of the 'accountability' of their behaviour. It is in this way that rules can have a normative force without having to be seen as internalized determinants of conduct.

> . . . Garfinkel's social actors were viewed as practical rule-using 'analysts', rather than as the pre-programmed rule-governed 'cultural dopes' portrayed by traditional sociological models of man (Atkinson and Drew, 1979, p. 22).

Thus it is not as a result of having internalized the rule that their behaviour comes off as guided by it. Rather it is their expectation that their co-interactants will take their behaviour, whatever it may be, as produced in reference to the rule. So if they want to avoid the implications that may be drawn if they are seen as violating the rule, they will design their behaviour explicitly so that it may be seen as conforming.

> . . . it is the methodic intelligibility of their actions which provides an environment of 'considerations' to which individual actors may orient in the design of their actions. Here the actor's primary concern may be with what is, in its double sense, the accountability of what they do. Compliance with the normative requirements of a setting may thus be most realistically treated not as the unreflecting product of the prior internalization of norms, but as contingent upon a reflexive awareness of how alternative courses of action will be analysed and interpreted (Heritage, 1984a, p. 309).

An important feature of this picture of the relationship between rules and behaviour is the emphasis it places on the temporal progression of action (i.e. on what the ethnomethodologists call the 'sequential relevance' of action). My behaviour is designed in light of what I expect your reaction to it will be: i.e. you will react to it as conforming to the relevant rule or as in violation of it, thereby leading you to draw certain conclusions as to why I violated the rule. An example which Heritage (1984a) discusses at length is that of greeting someone passing in the corridor. If you greet me, I am thereby put in a position of (a) conforming my behaviour to the rule 'return a greeting' or (b) failing to do so. In the case of the latter, because you hold my behaviour accountable, you will draw certain inferences to account for my rule-violating behaviour. You may infer that I did not recognise you, or that I was preocupied, that I simply didn't hear you, or indeed that I was purposely snubbing you or perhaps pretending, as a joke, to do so. Thus, by the inexorable fact that interactions progress, any component action inevitably is temporally situated in a sequential context, a context to which it is an addition and within which it will be interpreted, held accountable, and responded to in turn. It is because of this 'reflexive accountability' of their behaviour that

> . . . regardless of whether the recipient consciously 'chose' to respond in a particular way, he or she was nonetheless placed in a 'situation of choice'. This is so by virtue of the fact that actions reflexively and accountably redetermine the features of the scenes in which they occur. (. . .) The unfolding scene, in other words, cannot 'mark time' or 'stall' for a while; it will unavoidably be transformed (Heritage, 1984a, p. 107).

Related to the accountability of behaviour in interaction is the ethnomethodological notion of the 'architecture of intersubjectivity', the means by which individuals participating in the same interaction can reach a shared interpretation of its constituent activities and of the rules to which they are designed to conform.

> 'Shared agreement' refers to various social methods for accomplishing the member's recognition that something was said-according-to-a-rule and not to the demonstrable matching of substantive matters (Garfinkel, 1967, p. 30)

The view of intersubjectivity expounded by Garfinkel, and by the phenomenologist Alfred Schutz before him (cf. Heritage, 1984a, chapter 3), begins by stipulating the privacy or different individuals' experiences of their surroundings and the interactions in which they participate. Nevertheless, the inaccessability of the other's private experience does not prevent actors from achieving an intersubjective, 'shared world' as an ordinary, practical accomplishment. For, in interactions we operate under the common assumption that there are no interactionally relevant differences between our experiences and that, if some should arise, they will inevitably be made public through our own behaviour and its normative accountability. Once public, there are methodical ways of adjusting our understanding to bring them to a common ground that is 'identical for all practical purposes': i.e. similar enough for the practical demands of the present interaction. Thus, mutual, intersubjective understanding arises as an interactional accomplishment dependent on (a) our assumption that relevant differences will be made manifest in the interaction and (b) our interactional methods for recognizing and adjusting the differences that do surface. Both (a) and (b) may be seen to be dependent upon the reflexive accountability of sequentially ordered actions.

> . . . actors, despite their non-identical experiences and despite their lack of access to the full particularly of one another's experiences, can nevertheless proceed on the basis that their experiences are 'identical for all practical purposes'. Persistently conducting themselves on this assumption, a world of shared experiences—extruded, as it were, through language—is brought into being (Heritage, 1984a, pp. 59–60).

And, importantly, not only do actors succeed through the sequential progression of interaction to display their understandings of its constituent events and of the rules to which they are 'orienting', thus making possible the achievement of a shared interactional world, they also thereby make that shared world publicly observable to the investigating analyst of social interaction.

It may again be advisable to use an example to help clarify the ethnomethodological position on the sequential construction of intersubjectivity. Because interaction is reflexively accountable, an actor's response to another actor's behaviour will be taken as indicating the respondent's understanding of that behaviour. This 'display' of understanding by the responding actor may then, in the third position, be ratified or corrected by the original actor. So if, replying to your utterance, I said 'I'm sorry. I don't have a watch', I would thereby manifest my understanding of your utterance as a request for the time, an understanding which led me to design my own behaviour so as to conform to the rule 'reply to a request'. Just as important is the subsequent opportunity for you to correct or confirm my 'displayed' understanding of your original utterance. Thus, if you said in third position 'No, not the time, a *dime*' you would display your understanding both of my reply as well as of your original utterance and what would have been an appropriate response to it. A simple 'Too bad' on your part, however, would have confirmed my 'displayed' interpretation of your original utterance as a request for the time. By means of such a reliance on the reflexive accountability of actions situated in a sequentially ordered progression, actors may 'display' their own understanding and correct/confirm those of their interactants, thereby coming to construct a shared understanding sufficient for the practical purposes of the interaction. This construction we will call the '(sequential) architecture of intersubjectivity'.

> Linked actions, in short, are the basic building blocks of intersubjectivity (Heritage, 1984a, p. 256).

We may begin to put together the pieces of the ethnomethodological model of social interaction. Actors follow interactional rules (such as 'return a greeting') because they are aware of the interactional consequences of not doing so: in particular, they know that however they act will be held reflexively accountable by their co-interactants. The rules do not guide, or determine, their behaviour; rather they shape their expectations of what would be 'normal', i.e. what would be without need of special accounting. Actors may not have explicit knowledge of the rule which analysts would formulate as 'return a greeting'; but they are aware of the expectation that greetings will be returned and of the probable implications that will be drawn if those expectations are not fulfilled. Furthermore, this web of expectations, formulable in terms of interactional rules (or 'mechanisms', 'norms', 'systems', 'organization', 'devices': these terms are all used in the ethnomethodological literature with no consistently apparent differences) and the accountability of the actions to which they apply, provides the means by which actors can 'display' their own understanding of events and by which they may evaluate their co-interactants' understanding.

> Without a detailed texture of institutionalized methods of talking to orient to, social actors would inevitably lose their cognitive bearings. Under such circumstances, they would become incapable both of interpreting the actions of co-participants and of formulating their own particular courses of action (Heritage, 1984a, p. 292).

In addition to providing the theoretical backdrop against which the ethnomethodological study of conversational interaction must be seen, the principles of reflexive accountability and of the sequential architecture of understanding also provide the rationale underlying the analytical methodology of CA. Paradoxically, it is also because of this rationale that since the middle of the 1970s, ethnomethodological conversation analysts have been led to represent their discipline as methodologically self-sufficient, i.e. as independently coherent, without the support of its ethnomethodological roots. This has been a grave error, leading not only to a misrepresentation of the nature of the CA enterprise but also, which is perhaps worse, to a very general misunderstanding, on the part of 'outsiders', of CA methodology. As its practitioners published more and travelled to more conferences, CA attracted great interest, interest stimulated primarily by its wealth of 'empirical discoveries' about the details of conversational structure. However, at the same time, CA began not surprisingly to draw virulent criticism of its methods from other conversation and discourse analysts. Primarily, CA was seen to be unscientific and impressionistic (a claim some of the more polemical CA practitioners had already levelled at rival schools), as at best a preliminary, impressionistic assessment of conversational organization which, to have any real value, had to be followed by scientifically based studies using other analytical methods. This, in turn, has led to the growing isolation of ethnomethodological CA within the whole of conversation analytical studies and to a resultant increase in the misunderstanding both of the methods and of the findings of CA.

Nevertheless, it is our own firm conviction (and one which appears to be accepted by Heritage 1984a) that the CA methodology cannot be adequately understood without an appreciation of its grounding in fundamental ethnomethodological principles such as those discussed above. And the focal point of this appreciation, and consequently of its more common misunderstanding, is on the very question of the empirical nature of the methodology of CA.

> Conversation analysis in fact represents a vast extension—in both scope and detail—of the basic theorem of accountable action (. . .). According to that theorem actors may, or may not, act in accordance with the normatively organized constraints which bear upon them—subject only to the condition that 'deviant' actions may ultimately be recognizable, accountable, and sanctionable as such (Heritage, 1984a, pp. 291–292).

It is because of the accountability of interactional behaviour, and of the sequential architecture of intersubjectivity which it creates and sustains, that non-participant analysts are able to detect the nature of the actions being performed as well as the rules to which they are designed to conform. That is, because the interactant's own understanding of events is displayed in their subsequent responses to those events, and because those responses are either silently ratified or corrected by the producers of the original events, the professional analyst can obtain a clear grasp of the ways in which the participants themselves are analysing the interaction. The reflexive account-ability of actions and the related public display of understanding thus allows the analyst a view of the 'emic' categorization of events and sequences with which the participants themselves are operating. In this way, the eth-nomethodological conversation analyst employs analytical methods which are both 'emic' and empirical. They are empirical because the analyst does not have to rely on his/her own intuition in identifying a particular event or the rule which it is designed to obey, for the participants themselves manifest their identifications in their subsequent actions and reactions. In other words, the ethnomethodologist does not have to worry about imposing an analysis on the conversational data, for the conversation itself wears its (or the participants') own inherent ('emic') analysis 'on its sleeve'.

> The methodology employed in CA requires evidence not only that some aspect of conversation *can* be viewed in the way suggested, but that it actually is so conceived by the participants producing it. That is, what conversation analysts are trying to model are the procedures and expectations actually employed by participants in producing and under-standing conversation (Levinson, 1983, pp. 318–319).

> Thus the sequential 'next positioned' linkage between any two actions can be a critical resource by which a first speaker (and, of course, 'overhearing' social scientists) can determine the sense which a second made of his or her utterance (Heritage, 1984a, p. 256).

Conversational Mechanisms: turn-taking, adjacency pairs, and preferences

Armed with this empirical methodology, ethnomethodological conversa-tion analysts have, for over fifteen years, been investigating the details of conversational organization. Naturally, their discoveries are both too many and too complex to be discussed here at any length. Still, in order to give some substance to our discussion of the role of rules and units in eth-nomethodological investigations, we will give the very briefest sketch of a few of the major features of the CA model of conversational structure.

Probably the best known features are those termed 'adjacency pairs' and 'the turn-taking system'. In their article 'A simplest systematics for the organisation of turn-taking in conversation' (1974, 1978), Sacks, Schegloff and Jefferson argue for the existence of a 'turn-taking mechanism', having the function of assigning turns to the participants engaged in conversational interaction. In allocating a turn to an individual, the turn-taking mechanism initially allows the individual to produce at least one 'turn-constructional unit' (i.e. an utterance that is interpretable as recognizably complete).

> Instances of the unit-types so usable allow a projection of the unit-type under way, and what, roughly, it will take for a unit of that type to be completed. (. . .) The first possible completion of a first such unit constitutes an initial transition-relevance place (Sacks, Schegloff and Jefferson, 1978, p. 12).

The rules for the turn-taking system are as follows:

1. At initial turn-constructional unit's initial transition relevance place:
   (a) If the turn-so-far is constructed as to involve the use of a 'current speaker selects next' technique, then the party so selected has rights, and is obliged, to take next turn to speak, and no others have such rights or obligations, transfer occurring at that place.
   (b) If the turn-so-far is so constructed as not to involve the use of 'current speaker selects next' technique, self-selection for next speakership may, but need not, be instituted, with first starter acquiring rights to a turn, transfer occurring at that place.
   (c) If the turn-so-far is so constructed as not to involve the use of 'current speaker selects next' technique, then current speaker may, but need not, continue, unless another self-selects.
2. If, at initial turn-constructional unit's initial transition-relevance place, neither 1(a) nor 1(b) has operated, and, following the provision of 1(c), current speaker has continued, then the Rule-set (a)–(c) reapplies at next transition-relevance place, and recursively at each next transition-relevance place, until transfer is effected.

> (Sacks, Schegloff and Jefferson, 1978, p. 13.)

These rules are proposed as a formulation of the norms speakers and hearers 'orient' to in the management of the process of holding, securing, and giving up 'the floor' in conversation. Thus, it is hypothesized that by their 'orientation' to these rules and by the accountability of actions that fail to conform to them, interactants are able to produce the orderly exchange of turns that is so characteristic of ordinary conversations.

A noticeable feature of the turn-taking rules is their reliance on the notion of a turn involving 'the use of a "current speaker selects next" technique'. A typical instance of a turn employing such a technique is the first part of what it called an 'adjacency pair'. These are pairs of utterances (such as the greeting-greeting pair already discussed), the parts of which are regularly produced one after the other, although by different speakers. (Speaker A produces a 'first part', e.g. a greeting, and then Speaker B replies with a 'second part', another greeting.)

A basic rule of adjacency pair operation is: given the recognizable production of a first pair part, on its first possible completion its speaker should stop and a next speaker should start and produce a second pair part from the pair type the first is recognizably a member of (Schegloff and Sacks, 1973, p. 239).

Other purported types of adjacency pairs are invitation-acceptance/refusal, assessment-agreement/disagreement, self-deprecation-disagreement/agreement, accusation-denial/admission, summons-answer, request-acceptance/refusal.

The concept of the adjacency pair is, arguably, the linchpin of the ethnomethodological model of conversational structure. Not only, as we have seen, does the operation of the turn-taking system rely upon it, but also nearly every other structural feature so far identified by conversation analysts somehow incorporates the adjacency pair into its formulation (cf. 'openings', 'closings', 'repair', 'story-telling', etc.). And, at the same time, it is in the notion of the adjacency pair that the ethnomethodological principles on which CA is based are most usefully and obviously employed. Without the concept of the adjacency pair, there would be no ethnomethodological model of conversation; and in turn, without the ethnomethodological principles of accountability and of the sequential architecture of intersubjectivity, there would be no concept of the adjacency pair.

Heritage (1984a) argues also that, in the study of adjacency pairs, the methodology of ethnomethodological CA is best revealed.

> . . . the *form of analysis* directed to these very straightforward sequences . . . is repeated in the analysis of very much more complex, subtle and nuanced conversational activities. In each case, a 'current' action is analysed as projecting the production of a relevant 'next' (or range of 'nexts') by another speaker. When the relevant 'next' occurs, it is characteristically treated as requiring no special explanation: a relevantly produced next action is specifically non-accountable. (. . .) When the relevanced or appropriate 'next' does not occur however, the matter is, as we have seen, specially accountable (Heritage, 1984a, p. 253).

But as Heritage points out the concept of the adjacency pair should not be taken simply as the statement of an empirical regularity, or indeed of an invariant relationship. Reflecting the ethnomethodological principle of reflexive accountability, Heritage insists

> . . . we are here in pursuit of structural organizations which shape the expectations, understandings, and actions of interactants. (. . .) The adjacency pair structure is a *normative* framework for actions which is *accountably* implemented (Heritage, 1984a, p. 247).

It is important to remember here that the adjacency pair rule is not seen as a

determinant of the speakers' behaviour; rather it is a 'structural organization' to which the speakers 'orient' and which thereby 'shapes their
expectation' that the appropriate second pair part will follow the production
of the first pair part. In this sense, the second pair part (i.e. the sequentially
relevant next move) is 'accountably due', i.e. it is expected to be produced;
and if it is not forthcoming, interactants will look for some account for its
absence (e.g. the recipient did not hear the question, or is being rude, or . . .
etc.). A typical illustration of this picture of the operation of adjacency pairs
may be seen in the following extract from the transcript of a naturally
occurring conversation.

> T1   C: So I was wondering would you be in your office on Monday
>   (.) by any chance?
> T2   (2.0)
> T3   C: Probably not
> T4   R: Hmm yes=
> T5   C: =You would?
> T6   R: Ya
> T7   C: So if we came by could you give us ten minutes of your
>   time?

(From Levinson, 1983, p. 320.)

In this example it can be argued that the two-second pause following
T(urn)1 is the result of C's expectation that an answer would be forthcoming
from R to the question produced in T1. Furthermore, C's utterance in T3
('Probably not') can be taken as the manifestation of C's inference, drawn
on the absence of that expected answer. In other words, the pause shows C's
expectation that the answer was 'due'; while T3 shows C's expecltation that
its absence is accountable: i.e. that there is a reason for its absence. In this
case, the reason that C comes up with is that R will not, in fact, be in his
office on Monday and that he was delaying the provision of this disappointing information. (On the delay of 'dispreferred' responses, see below.) The
evidence in T2 and T3 can thus be taken as an indication of C's 'orientation'
to the adjacency pair framework (i.e. to the operative rule in this sequence)
and also as a sign of the reflexive accountability of all interactional
behaviour, even if, as in T2, the behaviour in question is simply one of
silence (R's non-response to the question).

At the same time we might also take this extract as an illustration of the
architecture of intersubjectivity in the identification of conversational
events. In T4, R says 'Hmm yes.' C's response in T5 ('You would?',
produced immediately following the termination of T4) then constitutes a
'display' of C's understanding of T4: i.e. it shows that C takes R's remark in
T4 to count as an affirmative reply to the question posed in T1, and not, for
example, as a confirmation of C's proposed response (T3) to the original

question. Given this interpretation, T6 may be taken as R's overt ratification of C's 'understanding display' in T5. Thus, the sequence T1–T7 may be seen to incorporate a sequentially constructed negotiation of shared interpretations. This is accomplished by means of the way each turn, in its context, displays its speaker's understanding of previous turns and of the rules to which that turn is designed to conform. This negotiation, of units and their governing rules, because it is 'displayed' in the turns themselves, both allows the participants to establish an intersubjective understanding of the interaction-in-progress and, at the same time, provides the conversation analyst with an 'emic' view of the interaction's developing structure.

An important component of ethnomethodological CA, related specifically to the notion of the adjacency pair, is that of the 'preference system'. In many cases, the first pair part of an adjacency pair will accept either of two possible second pair parts. For instance, an invitation has as its second pair part either an 'accept' or a 'reject'. In other words, the issuing of an invitation leads those who tacitly know the relevant adjacency pair rule to expect the next speaker either immediately to accept it or reject it. However, one of these two options will be 'preferred' over the other. We put scare quotes around the term 'preferred' because the ethnomethodologists claim not to use it in its ordinary sense relating to psychological motivations or desires.

> It must be pointed out immediately that the notion of *preference* here introduced is not a psychological one, in the sense that it does not refer to speakers' or hearers' individual preferences (Levinson, 1983, p. 307).

This is quite a controversial notion yet one which steadily gains more importance in the ethnomethodological approach to conversation analysis.

The most authoritative recent discussions of preference systems (Heritage, 1984a; Levinson, 1983) reach a consensus on how the notion of preference should be conceived. They point out that preferred second pair parts (e.g. the acceptance of an invitation) are typically produced immediately following the completion of the relevant first pair part (or even often in overlap with it) and without any special features of 'markedness'. Dispreferred second pair parts, on the other hand (e.g. the rejection of an invitation), are regularly accompanied by the characteristics of 'markedness'. By 'markedness' features, they refer to characteristics of dispreferred second pair parts such as

    (a) pausing before delivery
    (b) the use of a 'preface'
         e.g. (i) markers like 'uh' or 'well'
              (ii) token agreements, appreciations and apologies
             (iii) qualifiers

(c) the use of accounts, i.e. explanations for why the preferred second pair part is not forthcoming

(d) the use of a 'declination component': a form suited to the nature of the first part of the pair, but characteristically indirect or mitigated (Condensed and simplified from Levinson, 1983, pp. 334–335).

Apparently, the notion of preference systems, and of preferred and dispreferred second turns, is another consequence of the ethnomethodological practice of viewing interactants' orientation to conversational rules and structures as accountable. The production of a first pair part of a particular adjacency pair makes the subsequent production, by the next speaker, of the most appropriate second pair 'accountably due'. If the appropriate (i.e. 'preferred') response is not forthcoming, distinctive marking of the actual response produced can serve, at least, to indicate its speaker's acknowledgement of the absence of the preferred response and, thus also, of the dispreferred status of the actual response. Thus second speakers are seen to accompany the dispreferred second pair part with the characteristic features of markedness as a signal of their awareness of its dispreferred status, thereby acknowledging their orientation to the appropriate adjacency pair rule and to the accountable absence of the appropriate second pair part.

Thus, just as a question projects the relevant occurrence of an answer next, so an invitation projects the relevant occurrence of an acceptance next. And just as the failure to answer a question is accountable, so too is the failure to respond affirmatively to invitations . . . (Heritage, 1984a, p. 270).

The important thing to note in relation to the ethnomethodological notion of preference is that it is an essential part of the attempt to explain how conversational rules, such as the adjacency pair rule, actually come to influence (to shape, to design) the component utterances of the conversational sequences to which they apply. This is accomplished by the participants' knowledge that, at the very least, a displayed awareness of the relevance of the rule is required, even if it is not being obeyed. Hence, when speakers produce the rejection of an invitation they should somehow indicate in that rejection their awareness that what they should have done, according to the rule for invitations, is to accept. In this way, respondents may succeed both in achieving their own aims (e.g. by declining the proffered invitation) and, at the same time, in showing their continued desire to conform to the interactional rules which make conversation possible. All the while this is accomplished in a manner that is publicly displayed and therefore available for confirmation or correction.

Formalism vs. functionalism in CA

It is worth pausing to consider the concept of preferences in greater depth. Ethnomethodologists repeatedly insist that to say that one of two alternative acts is preferred to another is not to imply anything about the relevant speakers' own wishes, desires, motives, or the like. 'Preference' is not intended as a psychological concept, but rather as a technical means of referring

> to sequence and turn-organizational features of conversation (Schegloff, Jefferson and Sacks, 1977, p. 362)

and to

> describe the systematic features of the design of turns in which certain alternative but non-equivalent actions are taken, as well as aspects of the sequential organization of such actions (Atkinson and Drew, 1979, p. 59).

Recently, however, some of the leading practitioners of CA have begun to acknowledge that the differences between preferred and dispreferred actions cannot simply be reduced to distinctions in their formal design (cf. Owen, 1983, chapter 5; Heritage, 1984a, pp. 268ff.). Thus, more and more it is being accepted that preference cannot be a purely structural concept but must, to avoid incoherence, be re-interpreted under a functional explanation. It is easy to see why this must be so.

Indeed it would seem quite odd, even misleading, to retain the use of the term 'preference' to refer simply to formal differences in the design of alternative turns. For example, we may take 'I' to stand for the first pair part of an invitation, 'A' and 'R' to stand for its alternative second pair parts, accept (preferred) and reject (dispreferred), and 'M' to stand for the characteristic 'dispreference' markers. We may thus formulate the preference rules for invitations as follows:

If I occurs, reply with A or with R+M.

It is patently absurd to characterize such a relationship, seen, as some would wish, purely in formal terms, using the term 'preference'. Why, just because A regularly occurs without M, while R usually is accompanied by M, should this make A 'preferred' to R when following I? If sociologists were to observe that, following their entrance to a pub, customers either bought a pint of beer or bought a glass of spirits and some potato crisps, would they take this to mean that buying beer was 'preferred' to buying spirits? The chances are they would not, on the grounds that there is no obvious connection to be drawn between interactional preferences and bags of potato crisps.

Silly though this analogy may be, it serves not only to reveal the incoherence of interpreting the notion of interactional preferences from a purely structural perspective but also to indicate that there is more to the ethnomethodological use of that notion than the claimed reference to formal differences between alternative acts. For while there is no obvious connection between bags of crisps (as a dispreference marker) and preferences for spirts or for beer, there is a more obvious, though usually unacknowledged, functional connection between some dispreferred second parts to adjacency pairs (e.g. the rejection of an invitation) and the formal features of delay, mitigation, apology, etc., with which they are characteristically produced. And that is, simply, that their speakers would *prefer* (in the ordinary sense of the term) not to have been put in the position (by the first speaker's production of the first pair part) where they have to decline to produce the second pair part that the first speakers obviously would have preferred (again, in its ordinary sense) to hear. Consequently, they delay performing the act that they would rather not do, or they accompany it by an apology, or by an excuse, or mitigation, and so on. 'Preference' is, in fact, a perfectly appropriate term to use to refer to the differences between two alternative moves; what is inappropriate (not to say disingenuous) is to attempt to maintain the early ethnomethodological claim that those differences are purely formal, with no basis in the truly psychological or functional sense of 'preference'.

Still, the argument that preference relations have a functional and/or psychological basis has been hard for many ethnomethodologists to accept. Some, Owen (1983) and Levinson (1983) among others, have acknowledged its psychological function by tying it to the notion of interactional 'face', a concept derived from the work of Erving Goffman (cf. Goffman, 1967). Face is the image of oneself which, in interaction, it is assumed that participants work to preserve and expect their co-interactants to help them preserve. It is a form of externalized self-respect which Goffman believes much of the formal business of conversational structure is designed to protect. The formal differences between preferred and dispreferred second pair parts, it is suggested, may have just this function of preserving the 'face' of interactants. By showing my delay in rejecting your invitation, I display my hesitation to decline to do something you would prefer me to do. This displayed hesitation, then, is a sign of my continued respect for your 'face' and my desire (or 'preference', in its ordinary sense) not to damage it by my reply. Such a functional explanation of the formal characteristics of 'dispreferred' second pair parts appears to be gaining ground in the ethnomethodological literature.

However, it is worth pausing for a moment to consider why functional explanations of conversational organization have been so hard for ethnomethodologists to accept. The answer lies in the distinctive view ethnomethodological CA adopts of the ontological status of the rules of conversational organization. Note, in particular, the second sentence of the following quotation:

> The initial and most fundamental assumption of conversation analysis is that all aspects of social action and interaction can be examined in terms of the conventionalized or institutionalized structural organizations which analyzably inform their production. These organizations are to be treated as structures in their own right which, like other social institutions and conventions, stand independently of the psychological or other characteristics of particular participants (Heritage, 1984b, pp. 1–2).

In common with the other approaches to conversation analysis that we have looked at, ethnomethodological CA is based on the assumption that there are discoverable structural organizations (or 'rule systems', 'grammars', 'mechanisms', etc.) which are somehow the explanatory source of the observable regularities of conversational behaviour. Similarly, along with the other approaches, CA takes conversationalists to share a tacit knowledge of these underlying organizations. However, as a result of its ethnomethodological heritage, CA does *not* take these organizations and their constituent norms and rules to govern the conversational behaviour of those who have tacit knowledge of them. Nor are the rules unproblematically conceived of as 'generating' the behaviour that conforms to them. Rather, as we have already seen, conversationalists are held to design their behaviour so that it may be seen to accord with their co-interactants' expectations, expectations which have been formed as a result of their tacit knowledge of the rules of conversational organization. Still, conversationalists may well choose to contravene the rules, and in so doing to defeat their co-interactants' expectations; indeed, such rule-violations frequently occur. But in so doing, they know that their deviation from the rules will be held accountable. Thus, it is their awareness of the accountability of their actions which compels conversationalists to conform to the relevant rules. On that accountability hangs the ethnomethodological explanation of the regularity, stability, and normativity of the patterns observable in conversational behaviour.

It is important to see, then, that the structural patterns observable in a particular conversation and the rules of conversational organization are two different ontological entities. Neither is the 'output' of nor the 'generator' of the other. It is because the interactants involved in a particular conversation share a common, albeit tacit, knowledge of the rules and, thanks to their awareness of the accountability of their actions, act in accord with those rules that the conversation is produced in a recognizably structured form.

Obviously, it is essential in this case that the interactants in a particular conversation tacitly know, design their own behaviour to accord with, and hold others (and expect others to hold them) accountable to the *same* rules. These rules must be independent of the conversationalists themselves and their individual desires, motives, and eccentricities; and they must be relatively stable and context-independent. (This does not prevent the rules from being 'context-sensitive', as Sacks, Schegloff, and Jefferson (1978) point out. However, the manner of their context-sensitivity must be principled, stable, and independent of the 'psychological proclivities' of individual participants.) If you and I were 'orienting' to different conversational rules, we would not, consequently, act on the same expectations, nor could we hold each other accountable in the same way for the same actions. Since it is on the basis of these shared expectations and of our mutually enforced accountability that we may construct a sequential architecture of intersubjective, publicly available understanding of our interaction, a failure to 'orient' to the same rules would inevitably result in us being unable to co-ordinate our actions and our interpretations to the extent required for conversation to proceed. In other words, if we did not 'orient' to and hold each other accountable to the same rules, our conversation would collapse into misunderstanding and moral anomie.

> Without a detailed texture of institutionalized methods of talking to orient to, social actors would inevitably lose their cognitive bearings. Under such circumstances, they would become incapable both of interpreting the actions of co-participants and of forming their own particular courses of action. (. . .) In the absence of a detailed institutionalization of methods of talking, actors could not be held morally accountable for their actions, and moral anomie would necessarily compound its cognitive counterpart (Heritage, 1984a, p. 292).

Consequently, it is important to the ethnomethodological perspective that the rules of conversational organization be seen as ontologically independent of the private experiences, desires, and motivations of individual participants; for if they were not independent, there would be no guarantee that the resultant rules would be the same for all individuals, and conversational anarchy would be the result. It is for this reason, as the confusion over the concept of preferences illustrates, that ethnomethodologists shy away from a functional account of any mechanism of conversational organization. For the function that the conversational mechanism is designed to fulfil may not be seen from the same perspective in all contexts, by all participants concerned. For the same reason that Saussure sought to isolate linguistic structure from the caprices of time, of situations, and of speakers—that is, in order to explain the possibility of intersubjective communication—many ethnomethodologists seek to represent conversational organization as a purely formal structure independent of the functions it has to serve.

And yet, at the same time, there is a growing realization that, shorn of any functional motivation, the hypothesized formal organization risks losing its explanatory power. As we saw in the case of preference systems, such formal organizations may be taken as reducible to the observable, distributional regularities they were originally designed to account for. That is, if we disregard a functionalist explanation, the preference for A rather than R to follow I is reducible to the observable regularity that, when following I, R is normally accompanied by M, while A is not. Such a re-statement of the very regularity that the organizational device called a 'preference system' was designed to account for ends up draining the notion of a 'preference system' of all its explanatory power. One does not explain a regularity simply by re-stating it. It may well be because of their increasing awareness of these equal dangers, of a purely formalist perspective or of a blatantly functionalist perspective, that ethnomethodological conversation analysts such as Heritage are returning to the theoretical roots of CA in Garfinkel's dual principles of accountability and of the sequential architecture of intersubjectivity.

The Method Applied

Let us now turn specifically to the CA method of identifying the units of conversational organization and specifying the rules for their combination. These two operations are very much inter-dependent in the ethnomethodological framework. For a unit is identified (e.g. as an 'answer') by looking at its sequential context, i.e. at what it is combined with; and its role in that context (and thus its identification as a particular sort of unit) is determined by reference to the kind of sequence it is analyzed as (e.g. as a question–answer adjacency pair) Thus, whereas any specification of combinatorial rules will require the prior identification of the units so combinable, the ethnomethodological approach goes further in also making the identification of conversational units dependent on the specification of the conversational rules to which speakers 'orient' in constructing sequences of such units. At its worst, this might sound like a circular method of analysis, setting up a prototypical chicken-and-egg dilemma. But it may perhaps be better understood as an analytical consequence of the Garfinkelian theory that the fit between organization and phenomena, between rules and their applications, is not determined in advance, but rather is the result of an *ad hoc* and context-sensitive process, performed by speakers (by the use of shared 'methods'), in which the recognition of the social act and the construction of interpretation of sequences of such acts are two sides of the same creative (but nonetheless organized and accountable) process.

However, although we might convince ourselves that, in principle, this problem of analytical circularity is not as disabling as it might at first seem, it is however in practice, in the examples of conversational data we find discussed in the literature of CA, that the more serious difficulties reveal themselves.

Consider, for example, the following two examples, extracts from transcriptions of natural, spontaneous conversation. These are immediately followed by commentary from Heritage (1984a).

(1)

A: Whatcha doin'?
B: Nothin'
A: Wanna drink?

(2)

C: How ya doin'=
     =say what'r you doing?
R: Well we're goin out. Why?
C: Oh, I was just gonna say come out and come over here and talk this evening, but if you're going out you can't very well do that

Plainly the first utterance in each of these sequences is transparently prefatory to something (as it turns out, an invitation in both cases). Equally plainly each is understood as such by the second speaker. Thus, in (1), B's 'nothing' is not to be treated literally but as some kind of 'go ahead', while in (2) R's 'Why?' also attends to the prefatory character of C's enquiry (Heritage, 1984a, pp. 277–278).

However, it may not in fact turn out to be intuitively plain to all readers either that the first utterance in both (1) and (2) is 'transparently prefatory to something' nor that the second speakers understand them in that way. If we recall that the notion of the 'architecture of intersubjectivity' holds that a second turn will display its speaker's understanding of a first turn, then we should expect that, in identifying the first turns in the examples above, the analyst will refer to specific characteristics of their replies as indicative of the second speakers' understanding of them. Yet Heritage does not do this to support his claim about how the second speakers understand the first turns. Nor, significantly, is it clear what characteristics of the second turns might be taken as 'displaying' an understanding of the first turns as 'transparently prefatory to something'. In what specific manner, for instance, does a reply of 'nothin' ', to the question 'Whatcha doin'?', indicate its speaker's understanding of the question as 'prefatory to something'? The same point could be made about R's reply in (2). In other words, what we here lack is some sort of analytical criterion for justifying the analyst's reading of the replies as displaying some particular understanding of the first turn.

For another example, we might consider again Levinson's (1983) extract, which we reprint here for convenience.

T1   C: So I was wondering would you be in your office on Monday
           (.) by any chance?
T2   (2.0)
T3   C: Probably not
T4   R: Hmm yes=
T5   C: =You would?
T6   R: Ya
T7   C: So if we came by could you give us ten minutes of your
          time?

(From Levinson, 1983, p. 320)

Levinson comments as follows on this extract.

Here a two-second pause after the question in T1 is actually taken by C
to indicate a (negative) answer to the question. How can this come
about? Note first that . . . C has selected R to speak (. . .). Therefore
the two-second pause is not just anyone's pause or nobody's pause (i.e.
a lapse): rather it is assigned by the (turn-taking) system to R as R's
silence. Then recollect that adjacency pairs can have dispreferred
seconds, these in general being marked by delay (amongst other
features). Therefore the pause can be heard as a preface to dispreferred
response. Now in full sequential context it is clear that C's question is a
prelude to a request for an appointment, and for such questions it turns
out that negative answers (answers that block the request) are dispreferred. Hence C draws the inference from R's silence that he makes
explicit in T3. (That he got it wrong, as indicated by R in T4, does not
affect the point—such inferences are made, often correctly, though
sometimes not.) (. . .)

A fundamental methodological point can be made with respect to
(this example). . . . Conversation, as opposed to monologue, offers the
analyst an invaluable analytical resource: as each turn is responded to
by a second, we find displayed in that second an *analysis* of the first by its
recipient. Such an analysis is thus provided by participants not only for
each other but for analysts too (Levinson, 1983, pp. 320–321).

We have included nearly all of Levinson's analysis of this example
because it is an excellent illustration of CA method, providing clear
instances of its strength as well as of its weaknesses. The strength of the
analysis is that it seems to account for the occurrence of what otherwise
might be taken as the most trivial of conversational events: in particular, the
pause recorded in T2. Furthermore, by reference to such organizational
'devices' as the turn-taking system, adjacency pairs, preference systems and
the like, the analysis argues persuasively that, but for the speakers' mutual
orientation to these 'devices' and to the accountability of their actions, the
apparent coherence of this conversational extract would not occur.

And yet, it must not be overlooked how much these apparent analytical successes are dependent upon the analyst's stepping beyond the methodological limits allowed by the underlying ethnomethodological principles. Levinson claims, for instance, that the two second pause in T2 'is actually taken by C to indicate a (negative) answer to the question'. But is this really what C does? We might go so far as to grant that, in T3, C is anticipating a negative answer to the question in T1 (although there are other plausible interpretations of C's 'probably not' in T3). But even granting that, there remains no evidence *in the conversation itself* which shall lead us to conclude that C's anticipation of a negative answer comes as a result of his understanding *of the two-second pause* as indicating a negative answer. The only way that we may be led to that conclusion is by accepting the subsequent argument about turn-taking, adjacency pairs, and preferences. But this would be begging the question of the relevance of those 'devices' to an explanation of the behaviour of the speakers in the extract. In other words, it is not legitimate (1) to use the conversational data as evidence for the claim that it is by 'orientation' to those devices that the conversation develops as it does, when (2) the interpretation of the data itself depends on taking for granted the speakers' 'orientation' to those same organizational devices. For Levinson's argument to be valid, then, we need independent empirical evidence of how, in particular, C interprets the two-second pause in T2.

We may identify the general issue at stake here: whether the ethnomethodological principles of accountability and of the architecture of intersubjectivity, the principles on which the CA methodology is founded, can form the basis of practical analyses of conversational data. For instance, the principle of the sequential architecture of intersubjectivity holds that a turn displays its speaker's understanding of the preceding turn, a 'display' that allows both participants and analyst to check that they share a common understanding of the first turn. Applying this principle in practical analysis, Levinson takes T3 to display both C's understanding of T2, the previous turn, as well as C's 'orientation' to the adjacency pair preferences applicable to requests. Later, Levinson takes T4 to display R's understanding of T2 (pointing out that C was wrong in his interpretation of T2, 'as indicated by R in T4'). But no justification is given of the claims that T3 and T4 constitute displays of those particular interpretations and that those interpretations were reached as a result of C's holding R accountable for the two-second silence in T2. And yet, Levinson's analysis of the data hangs on those very claims. Why, we should ask, must we accept Levinson's interpretation of what T3 and T4 display? And, how could we know that that is what the participants themselves take those turns to display and that they reached those conclusions by means of their shared orientation to the rules of turn-taking, adjacency pairs, and preference systems?

The methodological prescription enforced by the principles of accountability and of the sequential architecture of intersubjectivity instructs the analyst not to identify the type of conversational unit instanced by an utterance solely by reference to its linguistic features (i.e. phonetic, morphological, and syntactic characteristics). Rather, the analyst is instructed to look to the turns following the relevant utterance; for those turns will display (for participants and analyst alike) the recipient's own 'emic' identification of the utterance (as for example, a question, request, etc.), the conversational rule(s) to which the recipient takes the sequence incorporating the utterance to be 'orienting', and the original speaker's own ratification or correction of the recipient's displayed understanding. Consequently, it is the conversational data itself which, by means of these 'displays', is to provide the analyst with the necessary criteria for identifying the conversational units being used and the rules by which they are being combined.

But what our discussion of these conversational extracts, and their analyses by Heritage and Levinson, shows is that this prescribed procedure, rather than offering the analyst direct access to the participants' own publically displayed identification of units and rules, only postpones the task to a subsequent turn. Instead of facing the problem of identifying the unit instanced and the rule oriented to by the utterance in the first turn, the analyst now has the task of identifying how the next turn 'displays' the participants' own solutions to that problem. But, as it turns out, this task is no easier than the first.

There are two responses to this problem, neither of which provides a satisfactory solution. The first is that adopted in the cited extracts by Heritage and Levinson, and indeed throughout the published ethnomethodological analyses of conversational data. This is to forego giving any criterion for determining whether a second turn displays an understanding of its first turn as an X, Y or Z, or as orienting to such-and-such a rule, and instead simply to provide an intuitive characterization of the understanding it displays. Thus, Heritage tells us that the second turn in (1) above 'plainly' shows the second speaker to understand the first turn as 'prefatory to something'. But, this is no more a satisfactory solution to the problem of identifying second-turn displays of understanding than it was to the original problem of identifying the acts performed by first turns. Indeed the inadequacy of intuitive characterization of acts as a basis of behavioural analysis is a characteristic ethnomethodological objection to alternative analytical frameworks.

The sociologist, having made his first-level decision on the basis of members' knowledge, must then *pose as problematic* how utterances come off as recognisable unit activities. This requires the sociologist to *explicate the resources* he shares with participants in making sense of utterances in a stretch of talk (Turner, 1971, p. 177).

It is not in their analyses of first turns that ethnomethodologists fail to follow these prescriptions, but in their analyses of the next turn's understanding 'displays'.

The second response to this problem is to accept in full, as Turner recommends, the methodological implications of the principles of accountability and intersubjectivity. This would entail accepting that the understanding of a previous turn displayed in a second turn is not something objectively given by the linguistic features of the second turn itself but rather remains to be decided by the conversationalists in subsequent turns. In other words, what understanding a second turn displays would have to be determined by looking to third and fourth turns to see what they take the second turn to have displayed: i.e. to see the understandings they themselves display of the second turn's understanding display. But, of course, the analyst could not simply read off the third and fourth turns' display of their speakers' understanding of the second turn but instead would have to examine subsequent turns for their displays, and so on. It is clear that the methodological implications of the principles of accountability can only lead to an infinite regress in which the function of any turn in the sequence A, B, C, D, . . . can only be determined by first determining the function of the next turn, which itself can only be determined by first determining the function of the turn following it, and so on. But not only would such a method of analysis be both endless and ridiculous, it also is obviously not what real conversationalists themselves do. Otherwise, they would have to wait until the final closing sequence of, for example,

    A: See you later
    B: See you later

to discover what they had been talking about!

In other words, the analyst, in attempting to apply in practice the principles of accountability and displayed intersubjectivity, is left to choose between (a) relying on intuition to identify the conversational work a turn is doing, a method the ethnomethodological approach was designed, at least in part, to improve or (b) abandoning any hope of identification, thanks to the infinite regress applying those principles entails. The latter choice allows the analyst to remain faithful to ethnomethodological principles but never to analyse conversations by a practical application of those principles; while the former choice constitutes an abandonment of the ethnomethodological approach just at the critical gap between theory and analysis, the very gap ethnomethodology was originally designed to bridge.

What is surely most frustrating for the conversation analyst convinced of the strength of the ethnomethodological picture of interaction is that the dilemma presented to the analyst by the practical task of applying its fundamental principles is obviously of no import to conversationalists themselves. They are not hamstrung in their efforts to understand what each other say by always having to defer their interpretations to a next turn that never finally arrives. If they were, then, given that they could never be certain what their partners were saying, conversational coherence would collapse. In conversations, we do feel that we understand what is being said to us and that we are being understood; yet if we were rigorously applying ethnomethodological principles we would not.

Conversation Analysis and Intersubjectivity

We might conclude this discussion of ethnomethodological conversation analysis by pointing out an assumption it shares with the more orthodox models we have so far studied. Both take intersubjective agreement, on the conversational units being used and on the rules being followed, to be the essential basis of the coherence and the detailed co-ordination of action that is characteristic of conversational interaction.

Orthodox conversation analysis holds that, for a conversation to proceed coherently, its participants must be predisposed to agree on the type of units instantiated by each of the utterances and on the rules governing the combination of those units. This occurs, according to the orthodox account, because the conversationalists recognize the 'distinguishing marks' which identify an utterance as a token of a particular type of unit and because they know in advance what the rules of conversation will allow as possible combinations of such units. Thus, their 'conversational competence' guides them in identifying and combining types of conversational acts.

The ethnomethodological approach, on the other hand, takes the crucial agreement on rules and units to be something for the conversationalist themselves to work out, *in situ*. The method of these negotiations relies on 'methodic practices' based on the principles of the reflexive accountability of interactional behaviour and of the sequential construction of intersubjective understanding. It is not a pre-programmed 'conversational competence' which guides them inexorably towards agreement, but rather the practical methods of situated, publicly displayed negotiation.

Our argument is that it is this assumption, shared by orthodox and ethnomethodological approaches alike (i.e. the assumption that intersubjective agreement on units and rules is a necessary prerequisite to coherent and co-ordinated interaction), that is the primary source of the problems encountered by analysts in trying to explain conversational data. It makes no difference whether that agreement is held to be the predestined product of competence or the outcome of public negotiation. In either case, the analyst is instructed to assume that all interactants see their interaction in the same way, at least as concerns the units and rules employed. The possibility is not entertained that this assumption may, from the very start, prevent the analyst from coming to grips with the true nature of the data.

For, is it true that, in order to avoid conversational breakdown, the interactants must be in (tacit) agreement as to (1) the functions of the constituent utterances as instantiations of particular organizational units and as to (2) the rules which apply to the combination of those units? (Note that for such a situation to exist, not only must the interactants agree on recognizing each utterance as a token of a particular type of unit, they also must agree on the taxonomy of units; for the former agreement would not be possible without the latter.) But what if persons A and B do not know, or even orient to, the same taxonomy of conversational units nor the same rules as applying to the combination of those units? And what if they do not recognize the utterances in their conversation as tokens of the same types of units? Will it necessarily mean that the conversation will break down into incoherence?

Before we attempt to draw general conclusions about this, we must focus our attention, not on another analytical model, but on an issue which concerns them all and which is also crucially relevant to the question just asked: how do conversational utterances relate to the grammatical sentences of a language?

7

Conversational Utterances and Sentences

Thus far we have considered various uses to which the notions of rule and unit have been put by a selection of models of conversational organization. But we have left until now the discussion of a further use, characteristic of all the models we have examined. This use is related to an assumption which appears to go unquestioned in conversation analysis: viz the assumption that utterances of conversational speech are related in a rule-governed way to the principal structural units of a language, that is its sentences. In other words, all the varieties of conversation analysis which we have considered take for granted a particular relationship between conversational performance and linguistic structure (and therefore also between the study of conversational performance and the study of linguistic structure). This relationship is epitomized in the assumption that conversational speech consists in the instantiation of linguistic units, i.e. sentences, and that these sentences possess structural and semantic properties assigned to them by the rules of the language in which the conversation occurs. Given this relationship between conversational utterances and sentences, the communicational characteristics of the former may be seen, at least in part, to be predetermined by the rules of the language. Thus, the analysis of conversational speech itself presupposes and depends upon a prior analysis of the linguistic units and rules of the language in which the conversation takes place.

Another way of expressing this commonly held assumption is to say that every conversational utterance is taken to be a token of a particular type of unit, the structural features of that unit being defined by the grammatical rules of the language. While this assumption is generally taken for granted by conversation analysts, few have considered the nature of the type/token relationship and the difficulties facing any attempt to provide an explicit formulation of it. Those who have considered it have usually reasoned that that relationship must be rule-governed, i.e. that conversationalists must, in some sense, 'know' rules which determine which sentence a particular utterance is a token of. This reasoning encounters difficulties, as a very few have seen, when presented with the considerable formal differences between many conversational utterances and the sentences they are held to instantiate. That is, many of the utterances produced in conversation show little resemblance to the sentences generated by the linguist's grammars. Realizing this, a handful of investigators have attempted to formulate 'editing rules', rules which provide a formal means of determining the sentence instantiated by any given conversational utterance. Given the obvious importance of editing rules to an account of the relationship between conversational and linguistic structure, it is essential that conversation analysts focus more attention on the possibility of the coherent formulation of adequate editing rules. Otherwise, we have no real grounds for assuming conversational speech to consist in concrete realizations of underlying sentential units. It is with this question that we conclude our survey.

Introduction

Any grammarian who has analysed a lengthy corpus of transcribed conversational speech will know that before such an analysis may be done, the data must be 'idealized'. That is, before the grammatical analysis may begin, the transcribed speech must be modified so that the utterances take on the appearance of sentences similar to those typically encountered in written discourse.

For instance, should the analyst come upon a typical stretch of speech like the following, he/she would not normally begin the analysis before making certain alterations to the text.

(1) It's just a subject which is— . sort of . basically well-known to all mathematicians and is a tool which . one uses whenever required and is—at the [ha:] . at the is the logical foundation of quite a lot of . quite a lot of things (S.1.6, 849).[1]*

To idealize this transcribed speech, the analyst will delete those parts of the transcription which keep the utterance from looking like a standard written sentence. For instance, the passage *and is—at the [ha:].at the is the logical foundation* would never appear in a written text. So, the analyst would probably idealize this passage to the form 'and is the logical foundation'.

Given the traditional support within linguistics for Saussure's principle of 'the primacy of speech', it is revealing to ask why the grammarian would decide to delete part of his spoken data so that it might conform to written language style. A contributory reason is that, according to conventional standards, the unidealized passage cited above is simply not grammatical. The sequence *and is—at the [ha:].at the is the logical foundation* could not

---

*Superscript numbers refer to Notes at the end of the chapter.

form part of what any grammarian would call a standard grammatical sentence of English. This is true regardless of the theoretical 'school' to which the grammarian belongs. Indeed, one part of the sequence, [ha:], could not be taken as a token of any word-form of contemporary English. Thus, to leave such a sequence unaltered in an utterance would render that utterance grammatically unanalysable. There is no need to go into the details of the various methods of grammatical analysis in order to defend this claim. Since the utterance both contains a form which does not approximate to any English word-form and incorporates sequences which could not form a part of any English sentence, it is clear that any grammatical analysis which takes the sentence and the word as its basic elements would not find the above sequence acceptable. One need only point to the odd combinations such as article plus verb (the is) and article plus non-word (the [ha:]) to confirm such a conclusion. Grammatical analyses are not designed to parse verbal sequences which are not sentences of English.

In his introduction to linguistics, Charles Hockett argues for such editing as a prerequisite to grammatical analysis (Hockett, 1958, p. 141). He produces a transcribed sample of real conversational speech. This sample, similar to the passage from the Lund Corpus given above, includes a typical amount of both filled and silent pauses, repeats, false starts and other features characterized by Hockett's expression 'hemming and hawing'. Following this sample, he offers an edited version of the same transcription. The edited version, from which the features of 'hemming and hawing' are deleted, is said to convey 'much the same meaning' as the unedited version. Indeed, Hockett argues, 'this edited version is implicit within the original'. It is such edited versions which Hockett claims to be the phenomena deserving of the grammarian's attentions.

> Recent research suggests that much can be learned about a person through a close examination of his unedited speech. The particular ways in which he hems and haws, varies the register of his voice, changes his tone quality, and so on, are revealing both of his basic personality and of his momentary emotional orientation. But since (if our assumption is correct) phenomena of these sorts are not manifestations of the speaker's *linguistic* habits, it is proper to ignore them in the study of language, basing that study exclusively on edited speech (Hockett, 1958, pp. 143–144).

Nevertheless, it should not be surprising that certain constraints are imposed on the grammarian's process of idealization. For instance, it is not within the grammarian's brief to render *all* ungrammatical utterances into grammatical sentence form. Furthermore, he must also edit sequences which, if taken *without* alteration, could possibly pass as grammatical strings.

(2) There be two girls at the door (invented).

Most grammarians will leave utterances like (2) intact in their analyses and will simply register the fact that, in the dialect being studied, (2) is standardly judged to be ungrammatical. Presumably, if similar usage of the copula was in fact found to be common, the grammarian might well question the standard claim of its ungrammaticalness. But s/he would never, for instance, edit it to the form (2a).

(2a) There are two girls at the door

To do so would be deemed a falsification of the data, a claim not ordinarily felt to be applicable to the type of editing Hockett recommends. So we may conclude that it is not merely the fact that (1) is ungrammatical that leads the analyst to edit it to 'ideal' form. Ungrammaticalness is not a sufficient condition to cause the grammarian to edit the form of conversational speech.

If we consider examples (3) and (4), we may see that ungrammaticalness does not provide a necessary condition either.

(3) I don't think. I mean he's very organized (S.1.8, 914).
(4) I'd paint for I'd paint forever if I had the time (S.1.8, 853).

In all probability, examples (3) and (4) would be idealized to (3a) and (4a) by the grammarian.

(3a) I mean he's very organized.
(4a) I'd paint forever if I had the time.

However, as they stand, (3) and (4) are not ungrammatical. If (3) was not altered, it could be analysed as the two sentences (3b) and (3c).

(3b) I don't think.
(3c) I mean he's very organized.

Similarly, the utterance transcribed as (4) could be analysed as the two grammatical sentences (4b) and (4c).

(4b) I'd paint for.
(4c) I'd paint forever if I had the time.

Thus it appears that there are criteria other than ungrammaticalness which may lead the grammarian to alter a transcribed utterance of conversational speech into an idealized sentence-form amenable to grammatical analysis.

The precise criteria which do, in fact, guide the grammarian's editing of 'raw' conversational data is a topic of obvious interest for the chronicler of practical scientific method, but it has little relevance to our present concerns. What does concern us is the use to which this picture of the practical grammarian's task has been put in the conceptualization of the connection between linguistic competence and conversational performance.

The target sentence hypothesis

In his article 'The production of speech', John Laver (1970) argues that 'hemming and hawing', such as that in example (1), is not noticed by the hearer in perceiving speech. Much like the analyst who deletes parts of a transcription in order to idealize it and thus make it amenable to grammatical analysis, the hearer is thought by Laver to 'edit' what he hears.

> The conscious perception of speech in some sense regularizes and idealizes the actual data of speech (Laver, 1970, p. 73).

A similar argument is proposed by Bernd Voss in a paper on hesitation phenomena and perceptual errors. He suggests that the hearer's

> idealization process is similar to the one operative in reducing speech to writing (Voss, 1979, p. 130).

The hearer is assumed to have 'in store' the units of the language and the possible sentential sequences of such units. So, when he hears an utterance, he attempts to take it as a token instance of one of the stored sentences. During the hearer's decoding of an utterance, then, he is thought to be forming hypotheses as to what sentence-type the 'incoming' utterance is a token of. If, having formed one such hypothesis, he can then take the remainder of the utterance as conforming to the predicted sentence-type, he will do so.

In this case 'performance difficulties' of the kind—*the logical foundation of quite a lot of . quite a lot of things*—would be unconsciously edited by the hearer in order that he might take the whole utterance (1) as an instance of the grammatical sentence (1b):

(1b) It's just a subject which is basically well-known to all mathematicians and is a tool which one uses whenever required and is the logical foundation of quite a lot of things.

That is, the hearer is thought to edit incoming utterances in much the same way as the grammarian who edits speech in reducing it to analysable, written form. By doing so, both hearer and analyst are able to assign a structural description to the competence sentence assumed to underlie the performance utterance.

A similar argument might be made regarding ellipsis. That is, in the same way that utterances including 'hemming and hawing', repetitions, non-fluency, etc. (all of which we will be referring to here as 'discontinuity'), might be thought to require the hearer to *delete* superfluous elements of the utterance in order to reduce it to grammatical sentence form, utterances involving the ellipsis of verbs, subjects, or other essential elements might be thought to oblige the hearer to *add* the 'missing' elements to the utterance in order to make it a fully grammatical, and thus comprehensible, sentence.

So, (5a) and (5c) would require their hearers to add various words in order to derive the underlying sentences (5b) and (5d):

(5a) In the car.
(5b) I left the keys to the house in the car.
(5c) Before.
(5d) Tom met Mary before he decided to devote his life to music.

Thus, while discontinuity can be taken to require editing in order to expunge superfluous elements from the utterance, ellipsis can be taken to require a complementary editing procedure involving the addition of missing elements. Both types of editing, under this view, would be essential to the hearer's need to derive the sentences underlying the speaker's utterances.

If we adopt this assumption (i.e. what will here be called the 'target-sentence hypothesis': that, like grammatical analysts, hearers have to edit incoming speech in order to analyse it in terms of its sentential grammatical structure), then it would appear that knowledge of how to edit utterances into sentences is an essential part of a speaker/hearer's conversational competence. That is, most hearers can be assumed to know that, in the appropriate contexts, a speaker's utterance of 'tomorrow' is to be edited to 'Tomorrow is my birthday' and that 'I saw Susan at—Mary at the debate' is to be edited to 'I saw Mary at the debate.' If they lacked this knowledge, it might be presumed, they would find much of ordinary conversational speech unintelligible. Furthermore, if we assume that hearers implicitly edit utterance tokens into sentence form, then we must also assume that, if all hearers of the same utterance edit it to the same sentence form, there are shared rules or procedures which guide their editing. Consequently, it becomes of interest to the study of conversation to determine what these rules or procedures are.

In this context the research on the perceptual errors made by non-native speakers of English takes on a relative importance. In the aforementioned article, 'Hesitation phenomenon and perceptual errors', Voss claims that his experiments show that non-native speaker/hearers of English have difficulties with the task of editing performance utterances into 'target' competence sentences. Sometimes they do not realize that editing should be done; sometimes they edit improperly; and sometimes they edit where no editing is required. Referring to the task of 'reconstructing' incoming utterances into appropriate sentence form, Voss claims:

> This, however, is a task which although usually no problem for the native speaker is typically more difficult for the non-native speaker. (. . .) The non-native speaker will find it difficult to know in each case whether a given stretch of acoustic information is part of the speaker's performance that can be disregarded, or whether, if the reconstruction is to be correct, it needs to be accounted for (Voss, 1979, p. 130).

In an experiment performed in 1975, Voss asked twenty-two German students to transcribe a passage of spontaneous English speech. All the students were training to be teachers of English and had undergone five to seven years of instruction in English. The experiment was based on the aforementioned assumption that speech perception consists of a matching between a predicted competence sentence and the incoming acoustic information. The students were asked to transcribe the passage

> as accurately as possible—in the sense of providing an orthographic rendering (Voss, 1979, p. 131).

It was assumed that the errors in the transcript—identified by a comparison of the students' transcriptions with a transcription made and checked by a native English speaker—should reveal the general causes of perceptual difficulties for the non-native speakers. In addition,

> No instructions were given how to handle hesitations. The assumption was that they would be idealized out. This turned out on the whole to be true . . . (Voss, 1979, p. 132).

Voss found that 32.6% of the errors made in the non-native transcriptions were

> likely to have originated in a misinterpretation of hesitation features (Voss, 1979, p. 136).

He groups the hesitation-linked errors into two types. The first type consists of cases where the subject has taken a repeat or a filled pause to be an instance of a word or a part of a word. For instance, the utterance *and you can—ring off a a great string* was interpreted by one subject 'and you can ring offer a great string'. What happened here appears to be that the hearer took the utterance of *off* followed by the repeated indefinite article *a a* as an instance not of a repeat but of a non-hesitation-interrupted sequence consisting of the two words 'offer' and 'a'. That is, the first *a* was taken as a second syllable attached to *off* to make the word 'offer'. Similarly, *a great string of erm of activities* was mistaken by one subject for 'a great string of an activities'. Here a filled pause is taken for the article 'an'.

The second type of error attributable to unfamiliarity with hesitation phenomena in English consists of those errors when the subjects mistook a word or part of a word for an instance of a repeat or a filled pause. Two cases are cited. In the first, the subject took the utterance *one of the problems—erm—of people who work* . . . for 'one of the problems people who work . . .'. Here the preposition *of* appears to have been mistaken for a filled pause and so was idealized out of the subject's transcript. In the second instance, the utterance . . . *such as—boat building* was transcribed as 'such as building'. Voss suggests that the subject here took *building* to be a correction of *boat*, since both begin with the same consonant. Thus the subject is supposed to have interpreted the utterance in the same way that one might (correctly) interpret the utterance *I work at the top of a large boat building on the 37th floor* as 'I work at the top of a large building on the 37th floor.'

In his own terms, what Voss's data seems to indicate is that the non-native hearers often did not know the signals given by the English speakers regarding when a section of the speaker's utterance needed to be edited or how it needed to be edited in order that it might match the appropriate idealized competence sentence. As Voss sees it, sometimes they edited where no editing was required, and sometimes they did not recognize cases where editing was called for. And yet native speakers do not appear to encounter these difficulties.

Consequently, if provisionally we accept Voss's reasoning, it seems possible to conclude that there are procedures which guide the hearer in establishing which competence sentence (or 'target sentence') a discontinuous utterance is to be matched with. The non-natives in Voss's test appeared to lack the linguistic knowledge required for the operation of these procedures. Furthermore, because lack of this knowledge seems to have kept the non-native hearers from performing as competently as a native hearer of English, this knowledge can, in some sense at least, be rightfully termed part of the 'knowledge of English'.

In this case it is not surprising that in recent years more attention has been drawn to the task of determining an explicit formulation of editing rules. Much of the recent interest in editing stems from a paper read by William Labov to the 1966 meeting of the Linguistic Society of America (Labov, 1966). In this as yet unpublished paper Labov argues that verbal performance is not nearly so ungrammatical as might be concluded from a superficial appraisal of conversational speech. By the application of a simple set of editing rules, it can be seen that less than 2% of conversational utterances are truly ungrammatical. Much of Labov's paper consists in the formulation of a possible set of such editing rules.[2]

A second source of recent interest in editing rules comes from the growing amount of money and research energy invested in the projects to develop computer programs for the processing of natural speech. If it will ever be possible for a computer to parse and interpret spontaneous speech, this achievement will require a program which incorporates editing rules. A recent paper by Donald Hindle (1983), an ex-student of Labov, proposes a set of editing rules to be incorporated into the computer parsing program 'Fidditch' developed by Marcus (1980). Of greatest importance to our purposes is the fact that Hindle (1983) adopts the now familiar assumption that any set of rules which can be shown to help a computer process speech must be similar to those used by the competent human language-user. Thus

Hindle's work on editing rules is intended as a contribution to the study of the editing rules human hearers use in transforming spontaneous yet flawed verbal performance into grammatical target sentences.

Why is the notion of editing rules, and the related target sentence hypothesis, so crucial to linguistics and to conversation analysis? The answer is that editing rules provide the necessary apparatus for linking a model of linguistic competence with the evidence of conversational performance. Without such a link it might be more easily argued that a model of linguistic competence, conceived as knowledge of the rules of a sentence-grammar, is irrelevant to an account of the everyday task of understanding conversational behaviour.

For linguistics standardly assumes that communication consists in the transfer of meaning from speaker to hearer and that this transfer is possible because the speaker and hearer share knowledge of the same abstract system fixing the relations between meanings and sentences, i.e. the grammar of the language. Thus by producing an utterance which instantiates a particular sentence of the language, I can be sure that, providing my hearer shares my knowledge of the grammar, he will understand my intended meaning. In such a picture of communication, much depends on the hearer's ability to establish the connection between the utterance I produce in conversation and the sentence of the language which encodes the meaning I intend to communicate. If my hearer cannot determine which sentence my utterance is supposed to instantiate, then my effort to communicate will be in vain. For communication to succeed, the hearer must be able to identify the sentence-type of which my utterance is a token.

Now, since communication only rarely breaks down, it seems reasonable to suppose that conversationalists generally have no trouble identifying the sentence-types of the utterances they hear. And, since hearers do not appear to have any trouble understanding elliptical and non-fluent utterances, then it seems plausible to suppose that they have methods for deriving the appropriate sentence-types from the elliptical and non-fluent utterances they hear. In this case the recent interest in editing rules is unsurprising.

However, if it should turn out that no coherent sense can be made of any hypothetical formulation of editing rules, then the manifest regularity of communicational success in conversation becomes evidence *against* the assumption that, in order to understand an utterance, a hearer must identify the sentence-type of which it is a token. And yet without this assumption it becomes unclear how a sentence-grammar model of competence can shed any light on the ability of humans to participate in conversation interaction.

Aims

Given this importance of the target sentence hypothesis and the reliance of that hypothesis on the notion of editing rules, it would seem essential to conversational study to discover a coherent formulation of rules for editing. The main aim of this chapter is to forestall any further research on such hypothetical formulations. It would be a waste of the researcher's valuable time. We will argue that no coherent formulation of editing rules could account for a wide range of utterances occurring in conversational speech, utterances which do not, however, appear to pose any problems of understanding for their hearers. To reach these conclusions, we will attempt to show that, in order to fulfil their function of deriving appropriate target sentences, editing rules must obey a variety of general constraints on their form. Secondly, I will argue that any proposed formulation of editing rules which *does* obey these necessary constraints will not be able to account for the evident interpretability of various types of typical conversational utterances. This double-bind will then lead to the conclusion that, since the target-sentence hypothesis relies on the notion of editing rules and yet that notion seems to be practically incoherent, the target-sentence hypothesis should be rejected.

In the following discussion we will focus our analysis on the formulation of editing rules for utterances with 'discontinuity' ('hemming and hawing', false starts, self-corrections, etc.). We will later argue that the obstacles to that task are basically the same as those facing attempts to formulate editing rules for ellipsis, although certain features of ellipsis exaggerate the difficulties.

Editing rules and their constraints

We may begin by identifying two phases in editing. We may imagine that the hearer is somehow able to determine both *when* an utterance should be edited as well as *how* it should be edited. Earlier studies of the editing of discontinuous utterances have assumed that speakers produce phonetic editing signals when their utterances require editing and that competent hearers have no trouble recognizing these signals. For instance, Labov (1966) assumes the speaker's editing signal takes the form of 'a markedly abrupt cut-off of the speech signal (which) always marks the site where self-correction takes place'. In order that we may turn our attention to the more complicated problem of formulating rules to guide the hearer in editing, we will ignore for the moment the issue of the editing signal. Let us assume for present purposes that speakers do produce editing signals when editing is required and that these signals consist in a discontinuity in the otherwise continuous production in the speech flow (i.e. 'a markedly abrupt cut-off of the speech signal'). This will then permit us to distinguish three components in the source utterance:[3] the discontinuity serving as editing signal, the speech prior to the discontinuity (hereafter the 'pre-discontinuity') and the speech subsequent to the discontinuity (hereafter the 'post-discontinuity').

It will be convenient in beginning this discussion to focus on one typical example of a discontinuous utterance in need of editing. In this way hypotheses may be easily formed and, if necessary, easily rejected before testing them against a wider range of data. Imagine a speaker producing the following discontinuous utterance.

(6) I've watched him for a long—longer than you have.

We might say that it is intuitively apparent that the target sentence for (6) is (6a).

(6a) I've watched him for longer than you have.

What sort of editing rule might we envisage for transforming (6) into (6a)? A first suggestion might be that the hearer simply compares the source utterance with a mental list of all the possible competence sentences of English. Indeed, sentence (6a) would be among the latter. However, how is the hearer to know which of many possible competence sentences is, in this instance, the appropriate target? There are other possible selections, such as those listed under (6b).

(6b) I've watched longer than you have.
    I've watched him longer than you
    I've longer than you have

If we assume that hearers do edit discontinuous utterances, then we must also assume that they have a means to tell *which* grammatical sentence is the appropriate target. Merely comparing the discontinuous utterance with a list of possible target sentences does not solve that problem. Furthermore, such an *ad hoc* procedure would permit different hearers of the same utterance to arrive at formally, and therefore semantically, contrastive target sentences. Given that discontinuous utterances do not often appear to result in communicational breakdown, then a method which leads different hearers to contrastive interpretations of the same utterance seems worthy of outright rejection. Editing rules must unambiguously pick out the appropriate target sentence.

It might here be argued that a hearer could easily select the appropriate target sentence from those possibilities listed under (6a) and (6b). This could be accomplished easily, because the hearer would already have formed an idea of what the speaker intended to say. There is a simple reply to this proposal: if the hearer can, in this way, determine directly from the speaker's discontinuous utterance and its context what was meant, then there is no reason for the hearer to perform the now superfluous task of editing that (already interpreted) utterance to target sentence form. If he has *already* understood, then any subsequent transformation of the form of the utterance would be pointless. The target sentence hypothesis is based on the assumption that a hearer needs to discover, by means of editing, the competence sentence underlying a discontinuous utterance and that the reason he needs to do this is so that he may then apply knowledge of the grammar of the language to derive the meaning from the competence sentence. There would be no need of editing nor of sentence grammars if the hearer could determine the speaker's meaning directly from the discontinuous utterance itself.

So far, then, we have come upon two principles governing any formulation of editing rules. They must guide the hearer unambiguously to the target sentence, and they must not presuppose the hearer's prior understanding of the utterance's meaning. We will refer to these principles respectively as the *principle of systematicity* and the *form-before-meaning principle*. As will later be shown, certain formulational constraints follow from these two essential principles of editing.

It is evident that in order to derive the target sentences (6a), an editing process is required which deletes certain units from the pre-discontinuity (here marked with an X):

(6c) I've watched him for X long . . . longer than
      you have.

We may imagine the hearer as deleting units from the pre-discontinuity in order to be able to take the post-discontinuity as a continuation from the pre-discontinuity, i.e. to take *longer than you have*, as a continuation from *I've watched him for*. The relevant question is: which constraints guide the hearer in his choice of elements to delete? Why should he not delete as in (6d)?

(6d) I've watched him for X long . . . longer
      than you have.

The result is a competence sentence ('I've watched for longer than you have'), but it is, nonetheless, not appropriate. In (6d) the hearer deletes too much of the pre-discontinuity. The deletion of *him* is in excess. The hearer also deletes unsystematically.

In deriving (6b) from (6), it would seem that a rule which might guide the hearer is as follows: delete 'from right to left' in the pre-discontinuity until the post-discontinuity may be taken as a grammatical continuation from the pre-discontinuity. The example (6c) conforms to this rule. The command 'from right to left' ensures a systematic order in the editing while the proviso 'until the post-discontinuity may be taken as a continuation from the pre-discontinuity' is needed to ensure that the deletion be the minimum necessary to arrive at a continuous grammatical sentence as target.

That is, to give one hypothetical description of the editing process, we may imagine that elements of the pre-discontinuity are deleted—starting with the last word and working back one by one to the beginning of the source utterance—until the remainder of the pre-discontinuity followed by the post-discontinuity approximate a satisfactory target sentence. Analogously, the source utterance can be thought of as a section of magnetic tape,

pre-discontinuity	post-discontinuity

We may then imagine that the post-discontinuity is pushed back over the end of the pre-discontinuity until a grammatical sentence, formed by the splicing of the two parts of tape, is arrived at.

ϕ a	b	c	d	e	f	1	2	3	4	5
I've	watched	him	for	a	long	longer	than	you	have	

discontinuity

So, first point (1) in the post-discontinuity is joined with (f) of the pre-discontinuity. But the resultant string—'I've watched him for a long longer than you have'—is obviously not a grammatical sequence. Consequently, the post-discontinuity must be pushed back further into the pre-discontinuity. If point (1) is made then to coincide with (e) in the pre-discontinuity, the resulting string—'I've watched him for a longer than you have'—is still ungrammatical. Not until point (1) (note: always the beginning of the post-discontinuity) is joined to (d) does the grammatical sentence (6a) finally appear.

The process may similarly be thought of in terms of deletion. That is, first the last word in the pre-discontinuity string is deleted, but the resultant combination of the remainder of the pre- and postdiscontinuity is ungrammatical. Only when the last two words of the pre-discontinuity are deleted—i.e. (d)–(f)—do we arrive at the grammatical sentence formed by (Φ)–(d) followed by (1)–(5).

It is important to note that the process deletes words of the pre-discontinuity in reverse order of their production and then stops as soon as a grammatical sequence appears. For instance, if this were not the case and (b) to (f) were deleted first, a grammatical sentence (6e) would appear.

(6e) I've watched longer than you have.

Similarly, deletion of (c) through (f) would produce a grammatical sentence:

(6f) I've watched him longer than you have.

Although there is hardly if any difference in meaning between (6f) and (6a), the principle that deletion proceeds one-by-one in reverse order of production (what will be called the 'minimalness constraint') must be retained so that grammatical but unsatisfactory sequences like (6e) are not derived by hearers.

At this point it seems appropriate to formulate the following hypothetical editing rule

Minimal deletion rule

If a break in the continuity of speech occurs,

(1) take the post-discontinuity as a continuation of the pre-discontinuity utterance, but

(2) If (1) is inapplicable due to its creation of an ungrammatical sequence, then delete only as much of the end of the pre-discontinuity as is needed to make (1) applicable, ensuring that the order of deletion is the reverse order of the production of the pre-discontinuity.

This minimal deletion rule is meant to apply equally to editing involving pauses, repetitions, insertions, corrections and other types of 'non-fluency'.

An examination of the minimal deletion rule reveals that it incorporates a certain number of constraints.

(a) *The minimalness constraint.* This constraint ensures that only as much is deleted of the pre-discontinuity as is required to allow the post-discontinuity to be taken as a continuation of the (remainder of the) pre-discontinuity. (There may, of course, be no remainder.)

(b) *The continuity constraint.* When the edit is complete, the post-discontinuity must be taken as a continuation from the (remainder of the) pre-discontinuity.

(c) *The deletion constraint.* The minimal deletion rule implies that any element of the source utterance which is deleted in the application of the rule does not form a part of the target sentence.

(d) *The grammaticality constraint.* This constraint ensures that editing is not complete until the (remainder of the) pre-discontinuity followed by the post-discontinuity forms a grammatical sequence, as defined by the rules of the language.

(e) *The identification constraint.* This constraint ensures that the minimal deletion rule is applied *if and only if* an editing signal, in the form of a discontinuity in the speech flow, occurs in the speaker's utterance.

The minimal deletion rule further specifies that all deletion proceed 'from right to left' in the pre-discontinuity. I will not insist on this constraint, as other editing hypotheses (e.g. Hindle, 1983) may have a different yet equally efficient way of constraining the order of deletion in the edit.

These five constraints, required by the more general principles of systematicity and form-before-meaning, form the obligatory basis of any coherent editing hypothesis. In order to support this claim, the following discussion will consider the need for each individual constraint.

Without the grammaticality constraint, there would be no need to edit any utterance. Speakers frequently produce discontinuities in their utterances where no editing of the pre-discontinuity is in fact required. We need only to think of the regular occurrence of hesitation pauses (cf. Maclay and Osgood, 1959), as in the examples below, to see that this is so.

(7) You're on this . [ə] senate committee of course aren't you (S.1.26, 1215).

(8) I don't know whether you . noticed (S.1.26, 1229).

Because these utterances are grammatical, though discontinuous, no editing of the pre-discontinuity is required.

On the other hand, were there no grammaticality constraint, hearers would never be led to delete any elements of pre-discontinuity sequences. That is, hearers must see that there is something 'wrong' with the syntactic form of an utterance, in addition to the occurrence of a discontinuity, for them to perceive the need for editing.

The continuity constraint is required to ensure that the hearer takes what comes after the editing signal (until a sentence boundary) as a *bona fide* part of the target sentence. Otherwise, the hearer might also delete the post-discontinuity, as in the following example.

(9) I've only got five years ~~to~~ [ʌ] eight years
~~to go~~ anyway (S.1.1, 315).

In addition, the continuity constraint ensures that the hearer knows how to put the remaining elements of the utterance 'back together again' after the process of deletion. Finally, the continuity constraint is itself presupposed by the minimalness and grammaticality constraints.

The identification constraint, as we have already seen, is required so that the hearer knows when (and when not) to edit. The hearer is not supposed to edit simply whenever s/he feels like it, regardless of the intentions of the speaker. Instead s/he must be constrained only to edit when the speaker produces an appropriate editing signal. Without such a constraint, the notion of a systematic editing procedure would be impracticable.

The minimalness and deletion constraints have been left until last because not all who have worked on editing agree on the need to constrain the hearer in these ways. For instance, the editing rules proposed by Donald Hindle incorporate neither of these constraints. The editing rules Hindle (1983) formulates amount to the following instructions to the hearer.

1. If an editing signal occurs and the surface strings on either side of the signal are identical, delete the first (as in example 10).

2. If (1) is not the case, but the two words on either side of the signal are instances of the same type of sentential constituent, delete the first (as in example 11).

3. If neither (1) nor (2) apply, go back into the pre-discontinuity until you find a constituent of the same type as the first constituent in the post-discontinuity. Delete the former (as in example 12).

(10) Well if they'd—if they'd had a knife I wou—I wouldn't be here today (Hindle, 1983, ex. 7a).

(11) I was just that—the kind of guy that didn't have—like to have people worrying (Hindle, 1983, ex. 8).

(12) I think that you get—it's more strict in Catholic schools (Hindle, 1983, ex. 9).

Perhaps the main problem with Hindle's proposed rules is that they do not combine the constraints of minimalness and grammaticality. Consequently, nothing tells the hearer (or the computer) which has identified an editing signal not to edit only as much as is required to obtain a grammatical target sentence. The point of these combined constraints is to keep the hearer from editing where no editing is required, in spite of the presence of an editing signal. For instance, Hindle's rules (but not the minimal deletion rule) would inappropriately oblige the hearer to edit the following (a) examples to the forms listed under (b), in each case because of the misleading presence of an editing signal.

(a) I suspected always that Delaney would be late . that Chomley would be on time and that this would *produce a nice staggering of their arrival on your desk* (S.1.1, 124).

(b) I suspected always that Chomley would be on time and that this would . . .

(a) This is to run their coordinating machinery—you know to establish the standards and all that kind of thing (S.1.1, 553).

(b) This is to establish the standards and all that kind of thing.

(a) And he was boasting about all this stuff they'd been using of Lawrence and . George Eliot (S.1.1, 837).

(b) And he was boasting about all this stuff they'd been using of George Eliot.

In addition, Hindle's rules would probably mis-edit the following example (13a) because it could not identify the constituenthood of the only partly produced form [bro:] and thus would produce the target sentence (13b).

(13a) *I've done mine and I . [bro:]* thought I brought it down (S.1.4, 243)

(13b) I thought I brought it down

Now, in one sense Hindle can accept (13b) as the target sentence for (13a), because he explicitly rejects the operation of a deletion constraint.

The status of the material that is corrected by self-correction and is expunged by the editing rules is somewhat odd. I use the term *expunction* to mean that it is removed from any further syntactic analysis. This does not mean however that (it) is unavailable for *semantic* processing (Hindle, 1983, p. 3).

In other words, Hindle can accept (13b) as the target for (13a) because he can always insist that, although deleted by the editing rules, the string *'ve done mine and I* is still available for semantic processing. Hindle cites the work of the ethnomethodologist Jefferson (1974) in support of the 'odd status' his rules assign to deleted material (Hindle, 1983, p. 3). In this case it is interesting that another member of the ethnomethodologist school of conversation analysis, Charles Goodwin, adopts the same fence-sitting position on the deletion principle. For Goodwin (1979), words in an utterance which are deleted through editing play no role 'in a unit on another level of organization necessary for properly understanding that stream of speech' (Goodwin, 1979, p. 98, fn. 3) (i.e. in the target sentence derivable from the source utterance). Nevertheless, much of Goodwin (1979) as well as Goodwin (1981) is concerned with revealing the interactional function of such deleted elements!

The fence-sitting position adopted by Hindle and the ethnomethodologists is incoherent for the simple reason that a verbal string cannot be deleted from the syntax of an utterance while remaining in its semantics. The argument in support of editing rules is based on the assumption that, in order to understand an utterance, hearers need to determine the grammatical sentence-type underlying it. If hearers *can* understand the meaning of parts of the utterance which do not function in the underlying target sentence, then there is no reason for them to edit in the first place. For they seem able to understand without the intervening aid of target sentence form. The result is that Hindle is left in the quite mysterious position of holding *both* that a hearer can understand, e.g. a sequence of five or six words to which his internalized processing programme assigns no syntactic representation, and that hearers need to edit utterances to grammatical sentence form *in order* to understand them.

It thus seems more reasonable to conclude that, if an editing hypothesis is to explain how a hearer equipped with knowledge of the grammatical sentences of a language is able to understand discontinuous utterances which are, at least superficially, ungrammatical, then the deletion constraint must be incorporated into any precise formulation of that hypothesis. The same is true of the minimalness constraint, which ensures that the editor only deletes the minimum that is required to produce a grammatical target. Nevertheless, it is not at all inconceivable that Hindle's editing programme could itself be edited so as to incorporate some version of the minimalness constraint. And his opposition to the deletion constraint is not essential to the formal coherence of his proposed programme.

There seems to be a strong case for incorporating each of the five listed constraints (as well as the two more general principles) into any proposed formulation of editing rules. Indeed, a proposal which failed to incorporate any one of the constraints would be incoherent or unworkable. For a wide range of the discontinuous utterances to which it was applied, such a proposal would either mis-edit the source utterance to an inappropriate target string, or, if it ignored the deletion or identification constraints, it would fail to serve the purpose for which editing rules are required, viz. to form an explanatory bridge between actual conversational performance and grammatical models of competence.

In spite of this conclusion, we will now argue that, essential though they are to any editing hypothesis, the incorporation of the aforementioned constraints would prevent any editing hypothesis from being able to account for the hearer's manifest ability to understand a wide range of typical conversational utterances. In this case, the very constraints which any set of editing rules must obey, if it is to account for one domain of the *explanandum*, serve to prevent those rules from being able to account for another domain of the *explanandum*.

We may begin by looking at the drawbacks with the continuity and deletion constraints. We have already argued for the need of these constraints if we are to conceive of editing rules as determining a systematic procedure for hearers to derive the underlying target sentences, and thus the meanings, of discontinuous utterances. However, the price of these requirements is that any set of editing rules which incorporate these constraints is not able to derive an appropriate target sentence (and hence a meaning) for the following sorts of examples

(14) That's . Velasquez' Pope Innocent the fourth . a copy of (S.1.4, 434).

(15) We could all slant atheistic slogans . slant . chant (overheard in conversation).

(16) The interview was-it was all right (S.1.3, 305).

The continuity constraint holds that, after all deletion has been carried out, the post-discontinuity is to be taken as a continuation from whatever is left of the pre-discontinuity. However, with examples such as (14) and (15) the appropriate target sentences, (14a) and (15a), could not be derived.

(14a) That's a copy of Velasquez' Pope Innocent the fourth.

(15a) We could all chant atheistic slogans.

Instead, because of the continuity constraints the sequences *Velasquez' Pope Innocent the fourth* and *atheistic slogans* would be deleted during editing. And, because of the deletion constraint, the semantic content of those sequences would not be derivable from the resultant target sentences. In fact, the continuity principle would prevent any edit arriving at a grammatical target sentence for (14). Thus, contrary to intuition, (14) would be uninterpretable to the hearer. Example (15) would simply be edited to *We could all chant*, leaving out the information regarding what would be chanted; and yet, again, it seems intuitively obvious that no hearer would experience any difficulty in interpreting (15) appropriately.

Example (16) poses a problem because, in order to arrive at a continuous, grammatical target sentence, the first three words of the utterance would be deleted in editing, resulting in (16a) as the target.

(16a) It was all right.

The objection to (16a) is that it does not provide the subject pronoun with an antecedent (and one does not occur in the preceding context). Consequently, given the deletion constraint, the intuitively implausible conclusion is forced on us that the hearer could not determine to what the pronoun refers.

In example (17) an edit under the constraint of the continuity principle would delete *not only*, producing the target sentence (17a). However, this target leaves out the first half of the *not only . . . but also* structure which does not seem lost to an intuitive interpretation of the utterance. Thus the deletion and continuity constraints seem here to produce a target sentence which is not an appropriate paraphrase of the source utterance.

(17) I'm very suspicious of the press generally and I can tell you because—not only I mean that's one case that you've given but also in their reporting of erm affairs foreign affairs . . . (example taken from Crystal, 1980, p. 158).

(17a) I'm very suspicious of the press and I can tell you because that's one case that you've given but also in their reporting of foreign affairs.

(In fact, the source utterance (17) appears to resist any systematic edit into an appropriate target sentence. This does not, however, make it any less easy to understand.)

Finally, in the following example the continuity constraint would ensure that the sequence *because of sessionals* would not occur in the target sentence even though it is intuitively relevant to an interpretation of the source-utterance.

(18) I had a seminar today in which people hadn't read the stuff because of sessionals hadn't read the play (S.1.4, 1082).

The minimalness constraint holds that *only as much* is deleted of the pre-discontinuity as is required to allow the post-discontinuity to be taken as a continuation of the pre-discontinuity. However, the minimalness constraint can often result in a target sentence which incorporates too much of the source utterance. Thus, this constraint would lead to (19a) and (20a) as targets for (19) and (20).

(19)   He's in the Yiddish [dipa:] department of Yiddish literature (S.1.2, 741).
(19a) He's in the Yiddish department of Yiddish literature.
(19b) He's in the department of Yiddish literature.
(20)   It was sort of the . . . uh certain speech patterns (example 9.3 from Labov, 1966).
(20a) It was sort of the certain speech patterns.
(20b) It was sort of certain speech patterns.

Although (19a) and (20a) are the grammatical target sentences that would be produced under the operation of the minimalness constraint, it is obvious that (19b) and (20b) would be more appropriate.

A similar situation may be seen with the following example.

(21)   It was during the fifty-six sixty-four (S.1.2, 1089).

From the context in which this utterance is embedded, it is apparent that the speaker means to say here 'It was during sixty-four', i.e. it was during the year 1964. Similarly, it appears from the context that the hearer understands that the speaker means 'during 1964'. But, if we suppose the hearer to be following a minimalness principle, s/he should not have derived a target sentence which could be so interpreted.

A strict application of the minimalness principle to (21) would merely result in the deletion of the pause between *fifty* and *six*. There is no reason why the speaker cannot be thought to be saying that the event referred to was 'during the fifty-six sixty-four'. To make sense of such an utterance we need only imagine that 'the 5664' refers to some event—e.g. the annual meeting of a futurist society. Similarly, if the hearer edits only *the* from the utterance, a next-to-minimal deletion, the target sentence—'it was during 5664'—makes perfect sense if taken within the context of a discussion of a science fiction novel about the 57th century. Or if the hearer deletes both *the* and *fifty*, a less minimal edit, the sentence would make perfect sense within a discussion of the remote past.

In other words, the minimalness constraint will sometimes impose too much of a restriction on the editing procedure. For the appropriate target sentence may not always be the first that the editor arrives at during editing. However, no satisfactory alternative method can be developed for constraining the amount of the pre-discontinuity to be edited. Hindle's constituency constraint (see our discussion above) sometimes deletes too much and sometimes too little. No other way to regulate the amount to be deleted in the pre-discontinuity seems possible unless we presuppose the hearer's advance knowledge of what the speaker intends to say. For instance, how can the hearer determine that (22a) is the appropriate target sentence for (22), even though a more minimal edit would produce the two complete targets in (22b), unless we assume that somehow he knows in advance that (22a) is what the speaker means? And yet if the hearer already knows, before editing, what the speaker means, then he need not bother editing.

(22)   If you take a statistical analysis of the people who pass you'll find that it is this question . which—they're passing on that question.

(22a) If you take a statistical analysis of the people who pass you'll find that they're passing on that question.

(22b) If you take a statistical analysis of the people who pass you'll find that it is this question. They're passing on that question.

Even greater than the problems arising from imposition of the continuity, deletion and minimalness constraints are those which arise from the identification constraint. The identification constraint presupposes, in general terms, that the hearer will apply editing procedures if and only if an editing signal occurs in the speaker's utterance. Furthermore, the identification constraint must assume that the speaker's editing signal takes some sort of recognizable phonetic form, specifically a discontinuity in the speech flow (a silent or filled pause, an abruptly cut-off speech signal, or some such 'hesitation filler' as *well, that is*, etc.). Hindle, for instance, recognizes the need for this constraint without stating how it can be satisfied.

> The self-correction rules specify how much, if anything, to expunge when an editing signal is defected. The rules depend crucially on being able to recognize an editing signal, for that marks the right edge of an expunction sight. For the present discussion, I will assume little about the phonetic nature of the signal except that it is recognizable, and that whatever their phonetic nature, all editing signals are, for the self-correction system, equivalent. Specifying the nature of the editing signal is, obviously, an area where further research is needed (Hindle, 1983, p. 4).

Two sorts of difficulties might arise as the result of the identification constraint. First, potential editing signals (however defined in phonetic terms) often occur where no editing is required, as in the following example.

(23)   And there was [em]—lecturer in German—a lecturer in philosophy—[em] . the president . of the college—the treasurer of the college—and another—bitchy . iceberg of a woman (S.1.3, 456).

However, provided we assume that the minimalness constraint operates, these examples should not raise problems for the identification constraint for, although the hearer will assume that editing is required whenever the appropriate phonetic signal occurs, the minimalness constraint will, in such cases as (23), prevent the deletion of anything more than the editing signal itself.

However, a more serious problem arises from the fact that editing is often required when no signal has occurred, as in the following examples.

(24) . . . and is—at the [ha:] . at the * is the logical foundation of . . . (S.1.6, 849).

(25) she said it's * the basic truth about men . is that men . like to be with other men (S.1.3, 755).

(26) And then they rang up about six months later * three months later (S.1.3, 134).

(27) I think * I think this is really [em]—this—feels fairly sound (S.1.3, 277).

(28) I could * I would * I had—joined the staff temporarily (S.1.6, 299).

(29) They've been offered accommodation in the college . which they've [teik] which they've actually going to * I don't understand American systems of . who pays for whose education (S.1.13, 284)*

(See also last example in section 4.5.1.)

At each asterisk in the examples above, editing is required, and yet no phonetic editing signal recognizable to the transcriptionists of the Lund Corpus occurs. Such examples are not hard to find; and yet their regular occurrence confounds the whole editing hypothesis. For how is the hearer, let alone a computer, supposed to know that such examples need editing and to determine where the editing should begin if there is no signal in the source utterance itself indicating its need of editing? Furthermore, if hearers can understand these utterances without being told that they require editing, then why should we suppose that, in order to understand utterances where discontinuities *do* occur, hearers must edit to grammatical target sentence form?

It would not be hard to argue that we have already seen enough problems with the minimalness, continuity, deletion and identification constraints to shatter any hope that a workable editing hypothesis might be constructed incorporating these constraints. The grammaticality constraint is inseparable from the other constraints for, much as the identification constraint concerns when to begin an edit, the grammaticality constraint formulates a finishing point for an edit. When enough deletion has been performed so that the remaining sections of the utterance may be combined to form a grammatical sequence of the language, editing is then complete. Thus, it is in order to achieve grammaticality that editing takes place, and when it is achieved, there is no further need for editing. The need for grammaticality, as we have seen, is based on the predominant assumption that speaker/ hearers know the rules for constructing and interpreting the grammatical sequences of the language. Thus, when a hearer is confronted by an ungrammatical string of words in an utterance, the only way he can succeed in deriving the meaning of that utterance is by first determining the appropriate grammatical sequence into which it may be edited. Thus we could not have a practicable editing hypothesis without the grammaticality constraint.

Nevertheless, we cannot have a practicable editing hypothesis *with* the grammaticality constraint either. For there are far too many utterances spoken in informal conversational speech which cannot be systematically edited to grammatical target sentence form and yet which intuitively seem easily interpretable and which do not appear to present their hearers with any interpretational difficulties. The following examples, which are by no means rare (cf. Brown, 1980; Crystal, 1980), provide instances of the sort of problems posed by the grammaticality constraint.

(30) It's just as good as setting Virginia Woolf and much more to where—these people want to read (S.1.1, 904).

(31) She said that affects the whole of living and the whole of the sort of [əm] you know going . I mean also of course this oil the oil heating (S.1.13, 357).

(32) But in actual fact of course their central heating oil . is probably roughly about the same price as ours because we're not [əm] for very cheap oil (S.1.13, 372).

(33) I mean I'm sack them (S.1.5, 646).

(34) How long do you suppose a life of a fur has (Brown, 1980).

(35) That is a suggestion for which I am all (Brown, 1980).

(36) I'm very suspicious of the press generally and I can tell you because—not only I mean that's one case that you've given but also in their reporting of erm foreign affairs (Crystal, 1980).

(37) Really unless there's something wrong with the candidate from their college . why she shouldn't get it . can you—this make sense to me sort of loyalty to their own (S.1.3, 266).

(38) We have some lovely moments when . a kid comes into court and he's got an air gun—and—[əm]—it's happened twice that [em] . they've been forgiven—and one time he was given an absolute discharge (S.2.13, 321).

(39) Now Sete is one of these beautiful towns that has . a little bit you known I mean your typical . sort of [əm] . Mediterranean . sea produce cafes and restaurants on the quay—and then . you go back sort of up you know the it rises steeply through you know sort of cobbled ways up . into the hills (S.2.13, 757).

(40) It's sort of very narrow streets and a forum and the rest of it and it's incredibly beautiful sort of spot that we've found (S.2.13, 777).

(41) The thing about Sete being not only is it quite an attractive . town—
     it's one of the . few places that had . at least four restaurants (S.2.13,
     785).
(42) It's built as heavily and . a . long time ago as it can be really (S.2.13,
     869).
(43) But it was quite a blizzard cause Sabre was out in the back garden
     and his huge Alsatian—I mean [riə] sort of covered in [s] . in in flakes
     of snow . it was really like a sort of beautiful wolf in the Arctic
     (S.2.13, 1049).

The point about these utterances, and the many others like them in
conversational speech, is that they cannot systematically be edited to
grammatical target sentences; nevertheless, they provide no real obstacles
to understanding (cf. Brown, 1980, p. 27). It is thus instructive to see the
logical corner into which such evidence forces proponents of any editing
hypothesis. They can say that the interpretability of such uneditable
utterances as these does not disprove the claim that hearers use editing rules
for simpler utterances. This is true. However, the question then arises: why
should they? If hearers have no trouble understanding such 'confused'
(from the perspective of grammaticality) utterances as (30)–(43) *without*
needing to apply editing rules, then why should we assume that to understand less 'confused' utterances hearers require the use of editing rules?
Hearers would then be viewed as some sort of very cantankerous cripples
who, although they have no trouble sprinting 100 yards in under ten seconds,
require the assistance of crutches when walking to the corner shop.

At this point there is an obvious strategy of rebuttal which the proponent
of editing rules will be tempted to employ. A familiar strategy in social
science methodology, it might be called the 'divide and conquer' method.
For it is open to the proponent of editing rules to argue that we have made
the mistake of grouping together two types of utterances, i.e. two domains
of the *explanandum*, which would be best treated separately. In other
words, it could be argued that it is unfair to take the resistance to systematic
editing by some utterances as evidence that a simple editing procedure,
obeying the constraints discussed above, is not in fact used by hearers to edit
more straightforward utterances. Such an attempted rebuttal would maintain that it is not inconceivable that hearers use one type of systematically
constrained editing procedure (e.g. the minimal deletion rule), for some
utterances and another as-yet-unformulated editing procedure for the more
difficult utterances. Our mistake, then, was in trying to formulate a general
editing rule accounting for all utterances.

The problem with such an attempted rebuttal is that it must rely on the
assumption that hearers could determine which set of editing rules to apply
to which utterances. They would have to know upon hearing an utterance

whether or not it should be edited by a rule incorporating (e.g.) the minimalness constraint. But how could they determine which rule to use unless they somehow knew in advance the intended target sentence? Since it would be admitting defeat for proponents of editing rules to hold that the hearer knows what the intended target is in advance of the choice of editing rule, their only recourse is to claim that the editing signal itself somehow indicates which editing rule is to be applied. However, the evidence of discontinuous utterances argues against this possibility, as do the example utterances listed above as problems for the identification constraint. For these utterances do not incorporate any editing signal at all.

The divide and conquer strategy not only presupposes that the hearer can recognize the criteria for that division. It also assumes that some sort of editing rules obeying the systematicity and form-before-meaning principles can be formulated for the more complex discontinuous utterances. But since these principles presuppose the five constraints discussed above, the evidence provided here argues against that possibility.

It is perhaps worthwhile at this time to glance at the complementary phenomenon of ellipsis. The obstacles which face any attempt to formulate rules for editing ellipsis are much the same as those for rules for editing discontinuity. Consider the following conversational extract.

T1　G.　I can't figure out how to start on a hill
T2　M.　By using the handbrake
T3　G.　And your left foot on the foot brake?
T4　M.　No, the clutch.

In each of the last three turns there is a great deal that the hearer would have to add to the utterance if, in order to understand it, s/he had first to edit it to grammatically complete sentence form. The second turn, for instance, would have to be edited to the target form (A), 'You start on a hill by using the hand brake' or something similar. But to arrive at this target sentence the hearer, in this case G, could not simply follow a formal procedure. For that might well result in the inappropriate target (B), 'By using the handbrake you figure out how to start on a hill'. In order to determine whether (A) or (B) is the appropriate target form, the hearer would need to determine in advance what M meant by that reply. But if s/he could do that then there would be no need to edit to grammatical sentence form, since the utterance would already have been understood and the edit would be pointless. Similarly, in order to determine whether the appropriate target for T4 is (C) or (D), the hearer would have to know already what M meant. A purely formal editing procedure, which did not rely on the hearer's advance understanding of the source utterance, could never determine which of the two was most appropriate.

(C) You start on a hill by using the handbrake and the clutch.
(D) You start on a hill by using the handbrake and your left foot on the clutch.

Indeed, it seems intuitively quite absurd to suppose that, in order to understand T4, a complete sentence such as (D) has first to be computed. It is revealing that this absurdity is the same many schoolchildren feel when they are told that they must not answer the question 'Who was the King of England during the American revolution?' simply by saying 'George the Third.' Instead, they are told to reply 'The King of England during the American revolution was George the Third.'

A similar dilemma faces attempts to formulate rules for editing ellipsis and rules for editing discontinuity. No comprehensive formal rules may be devised without relying on the hearer's prior understanding of the elliptical or discontinuous utterance. But if the hearer already understands the utterance, then there is no need to edit it to grammatical sentence form.

Grammaticality and communication

If the conclusion to the argument presented above is that hearers have no need of editing rules, then we can expect to be asked how hearers—without the help of editing rules—could make sense of ungrammatical, non-fluent and elliptical utterances. That is, the question will inevitably arise how can hearers understand such disorganized and incomplete utterances?

The first thing to remark about such a question is that it attributes 'disorganization' and 'incompletion' only to utterances which do not approximate to written language style. The question further privileges written language by assuming that writing is more transparently interpretable, i.e. less 'confusing'. The written language (or 'scriptist') bias has a long history in the study of language, and it reflects the continuing influence of the prescriptivism of traditional rhetoric on descriptive linguistics. In the present instance it leads to the assumption that the differences spoken language style exhibits, in contrast to written language style, are obstacles to spoken communication. So, since spoken communication is so regularly successful, hearers must have methods for overcoming those obstacles: e.g. by editing spoken language to written language form. In other words, the scriptist bias causes us to perceive a puzzle in spoken language and therefore also to seek explanations for how that puzzle never really poses a problem to conversationalists. The trouble is that the puzzle the scriptist sets himself appears to be unsolvable with the techniques of a linguistics based on scriptist assumptions.

In this case a better solution would seem to be to work towards a non-scriptist linguistics which does not take written language style to be the required form underlying all communicational expression. With regard to the questions of syntagmatic structure on which this paper has focused, the suggestions offered in Brown (1980) indicate the direction of at least one possible way to proceed.

In his article 'Grammatical incoherence', Keith Brown argues that hearers have little trouble understanding 'grammatically incoherent' utterances such as (30)–(43) above. The syntactic anomalies included in such utterances not only do not interfere with the success of the speech acts in which they occur, but also, he claims, they are probably undetected by either their speakers or hearers (Brown, 1980, p. 27). Referring to example (34), Brown presents a plausible argument in support of his claim.

(34) How long do you suppose a life of a fur has?

Having provisionally characterized the production of *a fur* as a cognitive blend, based on the model of *a hair* (the speaker is holding up one hair from the fur of an animal), Brown first hypothesizes that the surface structure of the whole utterance might be the result of the blending of the grammatical processes underlying the related structures (34a), (34b) and (34c).

(34a) How long a life does a hair have?
(34b) How long a life has a hair?
(34c) How long is the life of a hair?

Brown eventually argues against accounting for (34) in terms of a blending of the surface structures of (34a–c). This would be inappropriate, he says, because the mechanism which would be required to regulate such a blending would have to be very complex. It would be quite absurd to suppose that a speaker could not manage his speech production mechanisms well enough to produce a grammatically well-formed sentence yet could manage a complex mechanism required to blend three intricate surface structures into an ungrammatical output.

Instead Brown argues:

> It is perhaps less complex to hypothesise that what is involved is a set of abstract grammatical *processes*. The processes involved I have represented as 'interrogative inversion' (shared by (34a) and (34b)); DO support (shared by (34a) and the interpolated *do you suppose*), the formation of the correct form of *have* (shared in different ways by (34a), (34b)); the formation of constituents (shown by (34a), (34b), and (34c)). Suppose that some monitoring function is satisfied, if the appropriate processes have been carried out—and in a sense, as you can see, they have: we have DO support (but only once in *do you suppose* rather than twice), we have interrogative inversion, we have a form of HAVE, and we have the interpolation of *do you suppose* at a place that is consistent with some appropriate constituent break (Brown, 1980, p. 30).

data: it appears that two questions may be separated in the analysis of conversational speech: the question of communicational efficacy and the question of grammaticality. It is one thing to speak effectively, another to speak in conformity to the conventions for written language style. This does not mean that 'speaking grammatically' never overlaps with 'speaking effectively', but only that the satisfaction of the requirements for one does not imply satisfaction of the requirements for the other. With example (34)—as well as most of the examples included in this article—we have seen that one does not have to speak grammatically in order to speak successfully within particular communicational context. Similarly, we may imagine someone who speaks perfectly grammatical utterances 'worthy of prose', yet who fails to communicate in a situation because his utterances do not fit the communicational needs of the moment.

We have seen that to understand a non-fluent and ungrammatical utterance the hearer does not in fact need to transform that utterance into grammatical sentence form. The target sentence hypothesis and its subordinate apparatus of editing rules thus appear to be superfluous to any account of how communicational understanding is possible. Furthermore, the argument presented in Brown (1980) suggests that an account of the contribution made by syntagmatic relations to the communicational efficacy of an utterance does not need to rely on an intervening notion of grammaticality. This is certainly not the place to begin the exposition of a new theory of syntax, independent of the notions of grammaticality and sentencehood. In any case, there are a variety of ways that the requirements on such a syntax might be answered. Brown's suggestion of syntactic processes underlying the construction of an utterance is only one possibility. Others are conceivable; what is important for our present purposes is the understanding that the following two questions should not be equated.

A. How must language-users structure their output in order to make it grammatical?
B. How must language-users structure their output in order to make it communicative?

Both questions, it may be seen, demand contextually determined answers. How one answers the first depends on whether the output is spoken or written, telegraphed or shouted, used in an advertisement or in an instruction manual. The answer to the first also depends—as we all well know from letters to the newspaper and arguments with our friends—on who has asked and who is answering the question. But, finally, it is important to realize that in many situations—when the overriding concern is not grammar but communication—the first question is simply irrelevant, or, irrelevant until someone decides to make it explicitly relevant.

The same context-bound character must be attributed to answers to the second question. Whether an utterance is or is not a communicational success depends on who uttered it and on who they were speaking to. It also depends on what each interactant's criteria are for success at that particular moment and place. If a speaker inaudibly mumbles something and obtains the glass of wine he desired, this may be counted, in some situations, by some people, as a communicational success. Others may call it luck. But the point is that the question of the communicational efficacy of an utterance is not decidable once-and-for-all by fixed intersubjective criteria. The criteria change from interaction to interaction and from individual participant to individual participant; and the same criteria can be applied different ways in different contexts. In this case the answer to the question 'How must language-users structure their output in order to be communicative?' is not formulable in terms of abstract rules which generate all and only the set of communicative utterances. For what is communicative at one moment, for one person, may not be at the same or at a later moment, for a different person.

At the very least, the attempt to answer question B may be informed by a consideration of the prevalence of discontinuity and ellipsis in conversational speech. For this will show that the question of how a communicative utterance must be structured is not answerable in terms of specification of what the final verbal output must look like. An examination of the utterances that conversationalists actually produce leads instead to the conclusion that the final output can look like almost anything, i.e. that no fixed limits may be drawn determining what utterances must be like in order to be communicative. As our discussion of discontinuity suggests, in order to make their utterances cohere, speakers can draw on a potentially limitless range of resources: from gesture to 'paralinguistic' and poetic features and from situational context to assumptions of prior experience. For making one's utterance cohere is a fundamentally creative art, and that creativity is not explicable in terms of a simple choice between the instantiation of one fixed string of abstract elements or another. In the end nothing prevents the speaker from incorporating anything at all into his attempt to make his utterance cohere syntagmatically. The distinction, crucial to modern linguistics, between linguistic knowledge and non-linguistic knowledge and between linguistic and discourse or conversational structure can only serve to prevent the linguist from recognizing this fact. At the same time, we must not assume (we have no reason to assume) that the criteria according to which the speaker takes his or her utterance to cohere are the same criteria employed by the hearer. For the act of interpretation is no less creative than the act of speaking, and the creative act is fundamentally the act of an individual. Thus, the communicational efficacy, like the syntagmatic coherence, of an utterance is not only *not* determinable in advance, by the grammar of the language, it is also *not* determinable once-and-for-all for all participants and observers alike. The more linguistics enforces abstraction from time, from persons and from situations on its understanding of verbal behaviour, the clearer but, at the same time, the less relevant its analysis of verbal form becomes.

The linguistic perspective on non-fluent and elliptical speech provides only one example of this general law. Another is provided by the analysis of conversational structure in terms of abstract units and their combinatorial rules. The problem with analysing behaviour in terms of the instantiation of fixed strings of abstract elements, whether they be words or conversational 'acts', arises when one considers the huge number of communicationally successful strings produced which, under such an analysis, are incorrectly formed. This is the problem which a sentence-based linguistics encounters with discontinuity, with 'grammatical incoherence' and with ellipsis. The postulation of editing rules may thus be seen as an attempt to patch up the sentence-based analysis just at the point where it connects with reality: that is, at the point where the well-formed strings generated by the grammar are compared with the utterances produced and understood by real people in communicative interaction.

Within conversation analysis, Griceans and ethnomethodologists have sought to tackle the very same problem by developing new ways of conceiving of rules for the combination of conversational acts. The focus of the Griceans on normative principles and maxims and of the ethnomethodologists on accountability may be seen as products of the concern to bring together the abstract models of conversational organization with the creativity and spontaneity of actual instances of conversational behaviour. The linguistic analysis of syntax would do well to follow their examples. At the same time, conversation analysis should learn not to take for granted sentence-based syntax as the starting point from which the study of 'structure-above-the-sentence' is to begin. What research into conversation shows is that many of the basic assumptions underlying the study of verbal interaction, including those supporting such traditional linguistic domains as syntax, have to be reconsidered; and this reassessment must be performed in the light of conversation analytic discoveries about what speakers and hearers *really* do with words, and not just what grammarians, following an in-built scriptist bias, have for centuries been telling us that they do.

Notes

[1] All references in this form refer to specified tone units in Svartvik and Quirk (1979). The examples quoted have, to a certain extent, been simplified. In some respects this was unavoidable, given the specially designed typography used by Svartvik and Quirk. Our intention was also to make the examples as simple and readable as possible. All of the examples used are selected from speakers who did not know their conversations were being recorded. Further description of the conversations, their participants and the recording and transcriptional techniques may be found in Svartvik and Quirk (1979).

[2] Labov's paper may have been provoked by Chomsky's assumption (e.g. Chomsky, 1965) that one reason children could not learn a language by imitating the speech of their parents is that so much of adult verbal performance is characterized by ungrammaticality, self-correction, attention shifts, slips of the tongue and other such 'performance errors'. But if this is the spur to Labov's editing hypothesis, then it is perhaps understandable that the paper was never published; for it would have implied that, although children may not require the sort of innate grammatical knowledge that Chomsky assumes, nevertheless they must be assumed to have innate knowledge of something like editing rules. For how else are children to learn the editing rules required to correct the (superficially) ungrammatical utterances of their parents?

[3] We have chosen the terminological pair 'source utterance/target sentence' to suggest the parallel in translation studies to 'source language/target language'.

8

Conclusion

What conclusions do we wish to impart? Having found fault with each of the conversational models we have discussed, do we mean our conclusions to be entirely negative? If we are to commit ourselves thus, it is important that we make our meaning clear. What our discussions have shown is that every conversational model considered assumes conversation to consist in certain types of units, the production of which is governed by rules. It is this assumption which we take to be fundamentally misguided and to be the source of the conceptual, theoretical and methodological difficulties our chapters have revealed. Yet it is true that some models, in spite of the adoption of this rules and units approach, deal with these difficulties better than others do. Indeed it appears to be the problems that are raised by the rules and units approach which have pushed some ethnomethodologists to come up with novel perspectives on related notions generally important to conversation analysis notions, such as normativity, sequentiality and inter-subjectivity. However, we maintain that, until conversation analysis, including the ethnomethodological school, abandons its explanatory framework of units and rules, no rethinking of related concepts will be able to save the project as a whole.

This conclusion is best underlined by reconsidering the problems we have seen recurring for each of the models discussed. We have, for instance, repeatedly come up against the problem of identifying instances of particular conversational units (whether these are acts, moves, sentences, repairs, first pair parts, etc). To deal with this problem analysts have attempted to develop either 'etic' or 'emic' identificational criteria. In the former case, however, no convincing argument has been provided to show that the units identified by 'etic' criteria are those which are relevant to the conversationalists' own perceptions and to their own construction of a conversation. Thus, an excess in descriptive precision results in a lack of analytical relevance. As regards 'emic' identificational criteria, we hope to have uncovered what appear to be the insuperable methodological obstacles facing any attempt to apply such criteria in the practical analysis of conversational data. In the end, such attempts lead either to an unjustifiable reliance on the analyst's own intuitions or to the sort of infinite regress exemplified in the ethnomethodologist's search for 'displays' of understanding. Indeed, the 'emic' approaches lead us to raise the question whether participants in a conversation do in fact perform a shared identification of stretches of behaviour as tokens of particular types of conversational units. The importance of this question cannot be exaggerated, especially if our conclusions about editing rules and the structure/performance dichotomy are taken into account. If we abandon the assumption that conversationalists do perform a shared identification of units (an assumption which is foundational to the rules and units approaches), then the need to develop analytical criteria for identifying those units disappears.

Another issue we have seen recurring in our discussions is the need to distinguish 'free' regularities from rule-governed regularities. If it is accepted that some regularities in conversational behaviour are not rule-governed, then it becomes essential to distinguish between those that are and those that are not. We hope to have shown that many of the behavioural patterns for which conversational analysts have tried to provide rule-based explanations could be more simply explained without rules. This problem leads directly to more general conceptual confusions, endemic to the social sciences and philosophy, about the nature of rules and about what it means to follow a rule (see Baker and Hacker, 1984a, 1984b). We see a need for a stricter application of the concepts of rules and rule-following in conversation analysis. It may well be that the best conclusion is that it is inappropriate, even incoherent, to speak of conversational interaction as a rule-governed activity.

At this point it is worth asking why the rules and units approach has been so popular. The fact that so many differing theories of the types of conversational units and of the nature and status of conversational rules have proliferated during the short history of conversation analysis shows that there has been a growing realization of the theoretical and methodological problems in explaining conversational organization in terms of units and rules; but this has not yet led to the abandonment of that explanatory approach. Why not?

Undoubtedly, one of the main reasons for the persistence of the rules and units approach is that it is an imitation of the approach perceived as being highly successful in general linguistics. The linguistic study of verbal behaviour takes that behaviour to consist in the production of different types of identifiable units (depending on the level of analysis, phonemes, morphemes, words, phrases, etc.). Furthermore, modern linguistics is held to have had considerable success formulating the rules by which, at each level, such units may be combined to form grammatical sequences. Just as discourse and conversational units such as the speech act and the move were thought at one time to be units of linguistic structure, though not necessarily co-extensive with the sentence or clause, it was also assumed that rules similar to those formulated for grammatical analysis could be formulated to account for acceptable sequences of conversational units. The distributional approach of Zellig Harris is a good example of this overt concern to extend the rules and units approach beyond the sentence. And this type of distributionalism can be seen as a continuing influence in many of the studies we have considered in this book: in the work of Clarke, of Labov and Fanshel, of the discourse analysts of the Birmingham school and the less functionally-oriented of the ethnomethodologists.

Nor can we discount the influence of the social scientist's respect for formalism generally. The rules and units approach lends itself easily to the formalization of descriptive statements. Because of the perceived simplicity and systematicity of formalized descriptions, it is a common (but lamentable) tendency to attribute knowledge of the formulae to the actors whose behaviour was at first the object of formal description. Then, it is an equally common practice to make the epistemological leap of assuming that the formulae actually govern the production of the behaviour itself: i.e. to equate descriptive formulae with normative rules (or generative processes!). Thus, following a rule will be seen as the same thing as acting in conformity with a description. These tendencies are well illustrated in our central chapters as well as in the history of modern linguistics.

The rules and units framework also draws much of its support from an assumption that is so central to the study of verbal communication in modern times it might be called its fundamental principle: the principle of intersubjectivity (or in the work of Roy Harris (1981, p. 9), 'the telementational fallacy'). According to this principle, communication is a means of bringing participants in it to a mutual awareness, a common perception, of an idea, an emotion, a representation, a governing structure and so on. Manifestations of the principle are to be found throughout the history of linguistic thought, and it is perhaps the strongest influence (and constraint) on the development of linguistic theory and linguistic methods.

Applied to the study of conversation, the principle of intersubjectivity leads to the assumption that speaker and hearer see a conversation in the same way: they see the same stretches of behaviour as questions, or repairs, or promises, or embedded noun clauses, or face-threatening acts. Furthermore, they take the rules applicable to the production and combination of such conversational units to be the same. That is, the possibility is ruled out, or at least ignored, that speaker and hearer have their own views of what is going on, what has happened, what is a next possible or probable event, and what it all means.

Given implicit (or explicit) acceptance of the principle of intersubjectivity, conversation analysis requires a rules and units framework—just as the telementational fallacy is inseparable from the related fixed-code fallacy (Harris, 1981, p. 10). For if it is assumed that speaker and hearer share a common view of their conversation, then conversation analysis has the task of explaining what that common view is and how it is arrived at. The rules and units framework provides the obvious answer: speaker and hearer share a common view of the conversation because they both know from what components a conversation may be constructed and how those components may be combined. Thus, shared knowledge of the possible units and rules which may compose the structure of any a particular conversation is what enables speaker and hearer to arrive at a common view of their interaction. We can agree on our interpretation of something because we know in advance what that something may consist of and the rules of its composition. In this way the principle of intersubjectivity leads directly to a rules and units framework, and the telementational fallacy directly to the fixed-code fallacy. Indeed, the rules and units framework is nothing but the application of the fixed-code fallacy to conversation analysis. As long as conversation analysis avoids asking questions about the nature and extent of intersubjectivity, preferring to maintain its belief in telementation, the rules and units framework will continue to dominate, and the problems it poses will continue to plague analysts trying to construct adequate models of talk.

Perhaps our most significant conclusion is that the differences between various models of conversation, so immediately striking when one surveys the field, are in actuality rather superficial. The diversity of conversation analysis can be traced in the end to what all models have in common: a need to manoeuvre around the problems which are posed by the rules and units approach. In our view, the only manoeuvre which is likely to solve this underlying problem is abandoning the principle of intersubjectivity from which the approach and its problems are derived.

References

Arnauld, A., and Lancelot, C. (1660) *Grammaire générale et raisonnée*. Paris.

Atkinson, J. M., and Drew, P. (1979) *Order in Court*. London: Macmillan.

Austin, J. L. (1975) *How To Do Things With Words* (2nd edn.). Oxford:

Baker, G. P., and Hacker, P. M. S. (1984a) *Scepticism, Rules and Language*. Oxford: Basil Blackwell.

Baker, G. P., and Hacker, P. M. S. (1984b) *Language, Sense and Nonsense*. Oxford: Basil Blackwell.

Boomer, D. S., and Dittman, A. T. (1962) 'Hesitation pauses and juncture pauses in speech', *Language and Speech*, Vol. 5, pp. 215–220.

Brown, K. (1980) 'Grammatical incoherence', in Dechert, H., and Raupach, M. (eds.), *Temporal Variables in Speech*. The Hague: Mouton.

Brown, P., and Levinson, S. C. (1978) 'Universals in language usage: politeness phenomena', in Goody, E. (ed.), *Questions and Politeness: Strategies in Social Interaction*. Cambridge: Cambridge University Press.

Chomsky, A. N. (1965) *Aspects of the Theory of Syntax*. Cambridge, Mass.: MIT Press.

Clarke, D. D. (1977) 'Rules and sequences in conversation', in Collett, P. (ed.), *Social Rules and Social Behaviour*. Oxford: Basil Blackwell.

Clarke, D. D. (1983) *Language and Action: a Structural Model of Behaviour*. Oxford: Pergamon.

Coulthard, M. (1977) *An Introduction to Discourse Analysis*. London: Longman.

Coulthard, M. (1984) Review of Scheinkein, J. (ed.), *Studies in the Organization of Conversational Interaction*. *Language in Society*, Vol. 13, pp. 363–369.

Coulthard, M., and Montgomery, M. (1981) *Studies in Discourse Analysis*. London: Routledge & Kegan Paul.

Coulthard, M., Montgomery, M. and Brazil, D. (1981) 'Developing a description of spoken discourse', in Coulthard, M., and Montgomery, M. (eds.), *Studies in Discourse Analysis*. London: Routledge & Kegan Paul.

Crystal, D. (1980) 'Neglected factors in conversational English', in Greenbaum, S., Leech, G., and Svartvik, J. (eds.), *Studies in English Linguistics for Randolph Quirk*. London: Longman.

Duncan, S., and Fiske, D. W. (1977) *Face-to-Face Interaction: Research, Methods and Theory*. Hillsdale, N.J.: Erlbaum.

Edmondson, W. (1981) *Spoken Discourse, A Model for Analysis*. London: Longman.

Fawcett, R. (1980) *Cognitive Linguistics and Social Interaction*. Heidelberg: Groos Verlag.

Firth, J. R. (1957) *Papers in Linguistics 1934–51*. London: Oxford University Press.

Gardiner, A. H. (1932) *The Theory of Speech and Language*. Oxford: Oxford University Press.

Garfinkel, H. (1967) *Studies in Ethnomethodology*. Englewood Cliffs, N.J.: Prentice-Hall.

Garfinkel, H. (1974) 'On the origins of the term "ethnomethodology" ', in Turner, R. (ed.), *Ethnomethodology*. Harmondsworth: Penguin.

Gazdar, G. (1979) *Pragmatics: Implicature, Presupposition and Logical Form*. New York: Academic Press.

Goffman, E. (1967) *Interaction Ritual*. Harmondsworth: Penguin.

Goffman, E. (1974) *Frame Analysis*. New York: Harper & Row.

Goodwin, C. (1979) 'The interactive construction of a sentence in natural conversation', in Psathas, G. (ed.), *Everyday Language*. New York: John Wiley.

Goodwin, C. (1981) *Conversational Organization: Interaction between Speakers and Hearers*. New York: Academic Press.

Gordon, D., and Lakoff, G. (1971) 'Conversational postulates', *Papers from the seventh regional meeting of the Chicago Linguistic Society*.

Grice, H. P. (1975) 'Logic and conversation', in Cole, P., and Morgan, J. (eds.), *Syntax and Semantics, Vol. 3: Speech Acts*. New York: Academic Press.

Grice, H. P. (1977) 'Further notes on logic and conversation', in Cole, P. (ed.), *Syntax and Semantics, Vol. 9: Pragmatics*. New York: Academic Press.

Harré, R. (1974) 'Some remarks on rule as a scientific concept', in Mischel, T. (ed.), *Understanding Other Persons*. Oxford: Basil Blackwell.

Harris, R. (1981) *The Language Myth*. London: Duckworth.

Harris, Z. S. (1952) 'Discourse analysis', *Language*, Vol. 28, pp. 1–30.

Harris, Z. S. (1970) *Papers in Structural and Transformational Linguistics*. Dordrecht: D. Reidel.

Heritage, J. (1984a) *Garfinkel and Ethnomethodology*. Cambridge: Polity Press.

Heritage, J. (1984b) *Recent Developments in Conversation Analysis. Warwick Working Papers in Sociology*. Coventry: University of Warwick.

Hindle, D. (1983) 'Deterministic parsing of syntactic non-fluencies', *Proc. 21st meeting of the Association for Computational Linguistics*. Mimeo.

Hockett, C. (1958) *A Course in Modern Linguistics*. New York: Macmillan.

Jaffe, J., and Feldstein, S. (1970) *Rhythms of Dialogue*. New York: Academic Press.

Jefferson, G. (1974) 'Error correction as an interactional resource', *Language in Society*, Vol. 2, pp. 181–199.

Kreckel, M. (1981) *Shared Knowledge and Communicative Acts in Natural Discourse*. London: Academic Press.

Kress, G. (1976) *Halliday: System and Function in Language*. London: Oxford University Press.

Labov, W. (1966) 'On the grammaticality of everyday speech', unpublished paper delivered to the Linguistic Society of America.

Labov, W., and Fanshel, D. (1977) *Therapeutic Discourse*: Psychotherapy as Conversation. New York: Academic Press.

Lakoff, R. (1977) 'What you can do with words: politeness, pragmatics and performatives', in Rogers, A., Wall, B., and Murphy, J. P. (eds.), *Proceeding of the Texas Conference on Performatives, Presuppositions and Implicatures*. Arlington, Va.: Center for Applied Linguistics.

Laver, J. (1970) 'The production of speech', in Lyons, J. (ed.), *New Horizons in Linguistics*. Harmondsworth: Penguin.

Leech, G. (1983) *Principles of Pragmatics*. London: Longman.

Levinson, S. C. (1979) 'Activity types and language', *Linguistics*, Vol. 17, pp. 365–399.

Levinson, S. C. (1983) *Pragmatics*. Cambridge: Cambridge University Press.

Lyons, J. (1969) *An Introduction to Theoretical Linguistics*. Cambridge: Cambridge University Press.

Lyons, J. (1981) *Language, Meaning and Context*. London: Fontana.

McLaughlin, M. L. (1984) *Conversation: How Talk is Organised*. Beverly Hills, Ca.: Sage.

McTear, M. (1981) 'Towards a model for the linguistic analysis of conversation', *Belfast Working Papers in Language and Linguistics*, Vol. 5, pp. 71–93.

Maclay, H., and Osgood, C. (1959) 'Hesitation phenomena in spontaneous English speech', *Word*, Vol. 15.

Marcus, M. (1980) *A Theory of Syntactic Recognition for Natural Language*. Cambridge, Mass.: MIT Press.

Newmeyer, F. (1980) *Linguistic Theory in America*. New York: Academic Press.

Owen, M. (1983) *Apologies and Remedial Interchanges*. New York: Mouton.

Pike, K. (1967) *Language in Relation to a Unified Theory of Human Behaviour* (2nd edn.). The Hague: Mouton.

Ross, J. R. (1970) 'On declarative sentences', in Jacobs, R., and Rosenbaum, P. (eds.), *Readings in English Transformational Grammar*. Waltham, Mass.: Ginn & Co.

Sacks, H., Schegloff, E., and Jefferson, G. (1978) 'A simplest systematics for the organization of turn-taking in conversation', in Scheinkein, J. (ed.), *Studies in the Organization of Conversational Interaction*. New York: Academic Press.

Sadock, J. (1974) *Toward a Linguistic Theory of Speech Acts*. New York: Academic Press.

Saussure, F. de (1983) *Course in General Linguistics* (trans. R. Harris). London: Duckworth.

Schegloff, E., Jefferson, G., and Sacks, H. (1977) 'The preference for self-correction in the organization of repair in conversation', *Language*, vol. 53, pp. 361–382.

Schegloff, E., and Sacks, H. (1973) 'Opening up closings', *Semiotica*, Vol. 8, pp. 289–327.

Searle, J. (1969) *Speech Acts*. Cambridge: Cambridge University Press.

Searle, J. (1976) 'The classification of illocutionary acts', *Language in Society*, Vol. 5, pp. 1–24.

Shimanoff, S. B. (1980) *Communication Rules, Theory and Research*. Beverly Hills, Ca.: Sage.

Sinclair, J. McH., and Coulthard, M. (1975) *Towards an Analysis of Discourse: the English used by Teachers and Pupils*. London: Oxford University Press.

Sperber, D., and Wilson, D. (1986) *Relevance: Communication and Cognition*. Oxford: Basil Blackwell.

Strawson, P. (1971) 'Intention and convention in speech acts', in Searle, J. (ed.), *Philosophy of Language*. London: Oxford University Press.

Stubbs, M. (1981) 'Motivating analyses of exchange structure', in Coulthard, M., and Montgomery, M. (eds.), *Studies in Discourse Analysis*. London: Routledge & Kegan Paul.

Stubbs, M. (1983) *Discourse Analysis: the Sociolinguistic Analysis of Natural Language*. Oxford: Basil Blackwell.

Svartvik, J., and Quirk, R. (eds.) (1979) *A Corpus of English Conversation*. Lund: Liber.

Taylor, T. J. (1987) 'Alan Gardiner's *The Theory of Speech and Language:* Empiricist Pragmatics', in Harris, R. (ed.), *Linguistic Thought in England 1914–1945*. London: Duckworth.

Turner, R. (1974) 'Words, utterances and activities', in Turner, R. (ed.), *Ethnomethodology*. Harmondsworth: Penguin.

Voss, B. (1979) 'Hesitation phenomena and sources of perceptual errors for non-native speakers', *Language and Speech*, Vol. 22.

Winch, P. (1958) *The Idea of a Social Science and Its Relation to Philosophy*. London: Routledge & Kegan Paul.

Index